TEACHING FROM UNDERSTANDING

CRITICAL EDUCATION PRACTICE
VOLUME 15
GARLAND REFERENCE LIBRARY OF SOCIAL SCIENCE
VOLUME 876

CRITICAL EDUCATION PRACTICE

SHIRLEY R. STEINBERG AND JOE L. KINCHELOE, *SERIES EDITORS*

Teaching from Understanding

Understanding

Teacher As Interpretive Inquirer

Edited by
Julia L. Ellis

Garland Publishing, Inc.
A member of the Taylor & Francis Group
New York and London
1998

Library of Congress Cataloging-in-Publication Data

Teaching from understanding : teacher as interpretive inquirer / edited by
    Julia L. Ellis.
            p.   cm. — (Garland reference library of social science ; v. 876.
    Critical education practice ; v. 15)
        Includes bibliographical references.
        ISBN 0-8153-1166-4 (alk. paper)
        1. Action research in education.   2. Teaching.   3. Hermeneutics.
    4. Narration (Rhetoric)   5. Teacher-student relationships.
    I. Ellis, Julia Litwintschik, 1950–   .   II. Series: Garland reference library of
    social science ; v. 876.   III. Series: Garland reference library of social
    science. Critical education practice ; vol. 15.
    LB1028.24.N37   1998
    370'.7—dc21   98-23399
                                                                                                    CIP

Cover photograph depicting a mentor-student relationship by Lucy De Fabrizio.

Printed on acid-free, 250-year-life paper
Manufactured in the United States of America

to my parents
Monika and George Litwintschik

Contents

Acknowledgments

This book emerged from eight years of courses in which I invited pre-service teachers and graduate students to undertake interpretive inquiry projects in their practicum schools or work sites. Their work has helped me recognize the shape, process, and ultimate value of interpretive inquiry in pedagogic relationships so that I can confidently encourage others in this mode of research.

I am indebted to David Geoffrey Smith of the University of Lethbridge for my introduction to hermeneutics and interpretive inquiry. From his writing, speaking, teaching, and our many conversations I came to engage the ideas from hermeneutics as a way of understanding the world.

Graduate students at the University of Alberta contributed five chapters in this book. They originated as course papers or components of Master's theses or project research. I am grateful for the honesty and clarity of their writing, thinking and research and their willingness to share their work publicly.

Regarding my own chapters, I am grateful for the critical reviews of David Smith, Susan Hart and Ed Nicholson. I am also indebted to Ann Vibert and Nina Bascia for their encouraging responses to earlier drafts. I thank Tracey Kremer at the University of Alberta for her generous support and technical expertise during the preparation of the manuscript.

At the University of Alberta I had the good fortune to meet Max van Manen as a colleague. I already knew him as a prominent author. His encouragement and support have been extremely helpful, and I am grateful for his preface to this book.

I thank series editors Shirley Steinberg and Joe Kincheloe for their confidence, encouragement and imagination. Without their initiative, many projects like this one would never materialize.

Finally, I want to mention how much I learn from my family and how much I appreciate their humor, joy, good will and enthusiasm.

Julia Ellis
University of Alberta
August 17, 1997

Preface

Julia Ellis challenges us here to consider how a student experiences the classroom or any particular activity that is part of classroom life. It may be the most important challenge any classroom teacher can accept in all of his or her professional life. Teachers who orient themselves to their students' experiences are likelier to be in touch with them, both as individuals and as a class. Teachers who are in touch with their students take into account how children and young people experience life and how they understand, perceive, and feel about the material we expect them to learn. Only those teachers capable of such contact can distinguish what is appropriate from what is extraneous in their ongoing interactions with the students. Literally, each minute of the day teachers are on the spot, showing—by their actions, their glances and gestures, their silence and tone of voice—how teachers should be with their students. Indeed this constant pressure to say and to do the appropriate in the ever-changing context of classroom life separates the teacher as pedagogue from the teacher as mere instructor. In her work with novice teachers Ellis demonstrates her ability to draw student-teachers into the challenging question of how to understand their students.

Furthermore, she emphasizes that teachers must do more than ask what the students' experiences are like. Asking and answering the right questions while eliciting a student's experience demands of teachers a difficult pedagogical skill: the ability to sense the best ways to gain access to an understanding of young people's lives and then interpret what goes on in these lives. Through her insightful interview and observational practices, Ellis shows how student teachers can learn to interpret children's inner lives, thoughts, understanding, feelings, and desires from such questions as "What is the most difficult thing you've ever had to do?", "What would you like to be really good at?", and "What is the thing that worries you most?" Moreover, a teacher may gain access to what is going on with a student by observing such indirect clues as the child's gestures, demeanor, expression and body language. The student teacher as interpretive inquirer gradually learns to infer motives or cause-and-effect relations of classroom happenings. Such teachers can, as it were, interpret what belongs to the souls of young people, how they are the same and how they differ. The teacher learns to raise pedagogical questions: Is this a child who worries a lot? Is this a child who needs recognition? Is this a child who lacks self-confidence?

Ellis and her co-authors explain how teachers as interpretive inquirers can use interviews and creative assignments to access their students' realities. Moreover, since the interpretive task requires further refinement, they show how student-teachers may develop the perceptive ability to interpret the meaning of a child's worry, need for recognition, or lack of self-confidence. They lead us to other questions: What does this child's need for recognition have to do with friendships in and out of school? How is that child's learning affected by family circumstances? What is this child's relation to the teacher? To make pedagogical sense of particular situations with students, we must all learn how to interpret topic against theme, foreground against background, incident against context. Ellis's book demonstrates this hermeneutic dialectic with narrative portraits of particular students and teachers in relation with students. The portraits explore the interpretive significance of understanding the disruptive student, the student who reads with difficulty, the classroom climate created by a certain group of students, the special needs of individual students, or the experience of hard-to-reach students. These portrayals prompt us to reflect on the complex nature of teaching.

In reading *Teaching from Understanding* we meet many individual students and their teachers, and in the various stories and narrative accounts a strong theme announces itself and becomes a function of the interpretive process itself. As we orient ourselves interpretively to others, we see how important is the need for recognition in life. Children, young people, adults, and—yes—teachers too, want to be "seen." Wanting to be seen rather than ignored, the child talks out of turn, the student disrupts the class, the student-teacher keeps a journal, we all try to be acknowledged. The desire for recognition also means that we want to be seen as we feel we are. Here we find the interpretive challenge to be faithful to the interpretive responsibility of our relations with others. Many of us have experienced the unsettling predicament that arises when a teacher seems to see us differently from how we know we are, or from what we think we could be. It is a peculiar feature of pedagogical intentionality that teachers always expect more from students. Yet most educators realize that they should avoid expectations that, when challenged, some children simply cannot match. Aligned against this misrecognition of students' abilities, interpretive pedagogy includes the ability of "knowing" how much to expect. The teacher who believes in a student thereby enables that student to live up to the promise of recognition. We all want to be seen as promising and as capable of entering meaningful relations. We all want to be seen as worthy of respect, and we want to be seen as likable or desirable in our fundamental sense of self. These are the lessons the pedagogy of the teacher as interpretive inquirer can teach us.

Throughout this book, Julia Ellis and her colleagues bring the reader into a conversational relation with the question of the meaning of hermeneutics. They show how hermeneutics offers more than just a set of methodological techniques but also represents a responsibility that belongs to the teacher's vocation. As authors, they demonstrate how the act of writing fosters an attitude of reflective engagement with the data of our students' lives and worlds. Teachers who talk together about significant moments of their professional lives stand to gain much in interpretive insight. As teachers interpret their experiences in conversations with others, they learn about their own abilities to produce insights and understandings that make them more experienced and more action sensitive. But teachers who want to make sense of their educational lives with students need to do more than talk together. Ellis points out that teachers need to commit their interpretive impulse both to talk and to the act of writing.

This consequential act of writing differs from the moment of speaking in that we can weigh our written words: We can check their semantic values, we can clarify their meanings, we can taste their tonalities, we can predict and measure their effects on readers and on ourselves. In the practice of writing we can explicate and then bracket our assumptions, and we can compose and recompose our language and come back to the text again and again to get it just right before we commit it to permanent record. Thus, the experience of writing may lead to meaningful self-recognition: awareness of who we are and of what we are capable in our pedagogical relations with our students. In offering us an account of such writing commitments, Julia Ellis asks us to become writers ourselves. Teachers, student-teachers, and teacher educators can learn much from the interpretive hermeneutic of this marvelous book.

Max van Manen
University of Alberta

TEACHING FROM UNDERSTANDING

PART ONE

INTRODUCING INTERPRETIVE INQUIRY

Chapter One

Introduction:
The Teacher As Interpretive Inquirer

Julia Ellis

> *Carolyn was nearing completion of a unit on castles in her combined grades one, two and three class. She invited the children each to make a drawing of their ideal, fastasy home and to indicate who lived there with them. She then went around to the children asking them individually to tell her about their pictures and to say who they had with them in their fantasy castles. Most students named one or two favorite playmates and some included pets. Carolyn approached Melissa and her drawing with great interest. Melissa had been avoiding her friends lately and Carolyn had been trying to coax her back into being her old social self. Melissa's fantasy home-castle drawing was positive enough, but when asked whom she had in there with her, she answered "No one." At that moment Carolyn remembered that the child's mother had recently mentioned that Melissa was taking some special drugs for her asthma and there might be side effects. In the child's drawing and simple statement, Carolyn said she finally "heard" a six-year-old's articulation of "I just need some space right now."*

How does a student experience the classroom or any particular activity that is part of classroom life? Sometimes teachers feel they know or have a strong sense of these things and sometimes they don't. When lessons and activities roll along smoothly, questions about student perspectives may not be compelling. At other times, however, when teachers feel that things aren't going well for a student or for the class, or when teachers simply want more out of what takes place in the classroom, questions about students' experience can become genuinely preoccupying. When this happens, teachers often begin deliberative forms of interpretive inquiry.

Every teacher—in fact—every person is an interpretive inquirer. We interpret events, people, and objects in order to participate, interact, or behave in ways that make sense. When we are unsure how to interpret or "read" a situation, we try to explore further before acting or responding. We do most of this interpreting and exploring without a great deal of self-consciousness. In teaching, as in other aspects of life, when we are unsure what to do or learn that what we are doing is unhelpful or unwelcome we are jarred into taking conscious responsibility for how we have interpreted someone or something. At such times our exploring may become much more systematic and intentional. We can also become reflective and deliberative in considering how to interpret the "data" that result from our exploration. During this "research," we tend to be self-conscious about our efforts to develop and further our understanding so as to "see," "read," or interpret differently.

Writing has a significant role in this process of interpreting the data our explorations produce. In writing, we compose ourselves, putting our understanding together again in new ways. Writing invites reflection and deliberation: reflection on meaning as we search for the right words, and deliberation about the relationships among experiences or ideas as we evaluate the argument or interpretation we put forward in writing. Often, the insights and connections emerge from the very process of the writing itself. Thus, one can and should begin the writing without knowing everything one will say or write about.

Writing about their research can give teachers the chance to question, clarify, and extend their own understandings about their work with students. In this way, their research and writing becomes the source of their own professional development and curriculum planning. Teachers' written research can also teach others, including in-service and pre-service teachers, administrators and policy-makers, teacher educators, and parents. Only teachers themselves experience the questions and challenges of teaching and learning in the multifaceted, complex environment of the classroom. Only they can write about the kinds of understandings that emerge from experiencing that context in its wholeness. Others who wish to learn from these experiences can only access the thinking and feeling behind teachers' acting through teachers' own written explications.

When teachers and other professionals first consider the prospect of conducting research in their work sites, they often express concerns about "doing it right" and "using a correct method" in order to "be objective" and arrive at "valid conclusions" or make "accurate interpretations." These preoccupations are part of the legacy of the positivist and post-positivist traditions. The positivist research paradigm originated in the natural sciences where it was concerned with explaining, predicting and controlling. When this paradigm entered education after World War II, the ideal of research became the experimental design in which students were randomly assigned to experimental and control classes and the researcher manipulated an independent variable and then measured a dependent variable. The data from such studies had to be quantifiable in ways statistical analyses required. Research studies of this kind supported causal inferences and used the "grammar of science."

By the late 1960's a reaction against this paradigm emerged. As Husen (1988) noted, the great expectation for the scientific method had gone unmet as research findings still left people uncertain and confused. Behavioral and social scientists began looking to a qualitative, interpretive, hermeneutic, naturalistic paradigm. In doing so, they moved from a natural sciences preoccupation with "explaining" to a humanities interest in "understanding." These two forms of knowing had been differentiated by Dilthey in the 1890s.

In the post-positivist paradigm, qualitative studies relied on rigorously defined methodologies. Validity or truth was of great concern and one could expect findings to be valid if one had diligently followed procedures thought to assure rigor. The notion of validity in this paradigm assumed that there was a truth or a single reality "out there" to be captured.

Philosophical hermeneutics, elaborated by Gadamer (1989) in *Truth and Method*, has clarified that there is no reality "out there," no meaning or knowledge waiting to be disclosed to the "mind's eye," until the act of understanding brings it into being. Knowledge is the product of human activity. We create rather than find meaning or knowledge. Therefore, we can relinquish any fear that we will somehow miss finding "objective reality." Nor is a uniquely correct interpretation possible since perception is interpretation and each person perceives from a different vantage point and history.

Sometimes new researchers feel uncomfortable about the idea that their interpretations can count as knowledge. The prospect of this responsibility raises concerns about relativism since each person perceives differently. Each person, however, has a consciousness open to a reality shared in a community. As Greene (1994) observed, "modes of interpretation arise from a community" (p. 437). Moreover, each person communicates in language they expect others to understand: "To share in the world is to share in language" (Smith, 1993, p. 137). Consequently, a person's interpretations will rarely be bizarre or arbitrary, but rather will probably reflect an historical moment. To be concerned about relativism, wrote Smith, is to "confuse arbitrariness with historicality" (p. 138).

Beyond perspectives shared with a community, each person also has a unique perspective, since, as Merleau-Ponty proposed in *The Primacy of Perception*, perception "emerges out of our relations to situations and environments" (cited in Greene, 1994, p. 437). Today's postmodern precepts of situated knowledge, contextualized knowledge, and embodied knowledge represent a valuing of grounded knowing rather than a devaluing or dismissal of partial or perspectival knowing. By sharing the knowledge from each of our locations through dialogue we develop a fuller understanding of the places we inhabit together.

What one can see at any given time is limited by one's vantage point, or what in hermeneutics is called one's horizon. It means one's prejudices. Our horizons—our prejudices—continually change because of our contact with the horizons of others. Thus, the traditions that limit and influence us remain always in motion. To understand another, one does not surrender one's own standpoint and grasp that of another. Rather, as explained by Smith (1993), a fusion of horizons takes the form of broadening one's own horizon through "a dialogical encounter of questions and answers" (p. 137).

Hermeneutics also emphasizes the key role of language in understanding and interpretation. Smith's discussion of this point clarifies that language is more than just a tool; it is the very basis of understanding itself. A fusion of horizons takes place through the medium of language since our horizons are linguistic. Thus "the movement of horizons is the movement of language itself as the latter goes about its task of understanding" (p. 137). Since language and understanding are linked, no final or fixed understanding of ourselves or others is possible, just as there can be no fixed or final language to express our understanding. Understanding is always temporal, since, as our prejudices change and our language changes, so do the interpretations we can make.

At first it may seem discouraging to discuss the research process at all given that one's own interpretation may change over time and that others might describe the same phenomenon differently. Self-conscious research can, however, be an extremely creative and responsible activity. To begin with, the development of understanding amounts to the formation of the self. The key again lies in one's work with language in this process. As people more consciously and reflectively work on redescribing and reinterpreting, they exercise "the power of language to make new and different things possible and important—an appreciation which becomes possible only when one's aim becomes an expanding repertoire of alternate descriptions rather than One Right Description" (Rorty, 1989, p. 40, cited by Greene, 1994, p. 440). Greene insists that postmodernism allows no one truth, no single monological description of physical or human phenomena, and she suggests that to recognize this principle is "to become awake to the process of our own sense-making in a radically different way: to question technical and specialized authorities, to engage with intensified awareness in acts of becoming different, acts of redescribing and redefining ourselves and our contacts with our world" (p. 440).

Rorty (1982) suggested that as human beings we have only two projects: to take responsibility for our own continuing growth, and to contribute to solving the problems in our communities. In the latter project, he also focussed on the role of language, pointing out that throughout history most discoveries and advances became possible when individuals transcended the language currently available for thinking about the most intractable problems. The new language, or new conceptualization (often the result of cross-fertilization across disciplines when individuals moved from one field of activity to another), made it possible for others to imagine more fruitful approaches for addressing these problems.

Hermeneutical inquiry aspires to this kind of generativity. Research done in this manner may not necessarily provide the final answer to a question or a complete solution to a problem; rather it opens up promising directions for further inquiry or efforts. From interpretive inquiry we learn to think more fruitfully than we could before in our efforts to gain wisdom or find helpful approaches to difficult problems. The aim of interpretive inquiry is not to write the end of an existing story but to write a more hopeful beginning for new stories.

This book draws upon the work that many students and I have done with interpretive inquiry over the last eight years. In graduate courses, I invite students to undertake work site inter-pretive inquiry projects as part of their course requirements. Chapter 2 provides an overview of how we thought our way through this process. Chapter 3 focuses on narrative inquiry as a form of interpretive inquiry and reflects six years of narrative inquiries student teachers completed among students in their practicum schools. Using narrative inquiry with just one student, a pre-service teacher can learn a great deal about that particular student, about all students in general, about teaching and about themselves. Chapter 4 reports on my study of open-ended, self-expressive assignments student teachers use as a context for researching the students in their practicum schools. More than 450 student teachers completed this course assignment over a four-year period. This research process helped the pre-service teachers develop their understanding of their students and their opportunities to help those students.

Chapters 5 to 9, interpretive inquiry reports written by graduate students from the University of Alberta, illustrate and sometimes discuss the processes and principles discussed in these first two chapters. More importantly, they invite others to learn from these teachers' experiences and their deliberative inquiries.

In Chapter 5, Miriam Shell tells the story of her year with a young student who totally disrupted her classroom, her school, and her sense of balance. While Shell's inquiry began with a focus on understanding this child's difficulties, motivations, and needs, it moved quickly to a re-examination of her own beliefs to establish direction for her practice. As is often the case, the strategies she used to accommodate and support this one child made classroom life richer for all of the students. Shell comments on the supportive role her graduate studies played, offering opportunities for reading, dialogue with colleagues, and reflective writing. The paradigms and perspectives she read about and discussed gave her confirmation, clarification, and new language for expressing her experiences and aspirations. She found connection and community both with her graduate school colleagues and with authors and theorists in the larger educational community. Shell's new interpretive frameworks also gave her a way to articulate the new questions and concerns she identified.

In Chapter 6, Kathy Nawrot reports on discovering how children learn to read by studying just one child. Eager to help young students who struggle with reading in her classroom, Nawrot had taken graduate courses on reading but questions remained. In the research she reports here, she studied her pre-school niece every week for a year. She describes how her approach to her research gradually changed as the child demanded a human response and her own perceptiveness deepened and note-taking skills grew. In her discussion of the data analysis, Nawrot clarifies the role of the backward evaluative arc of the hermeneutic circle. In recircling through all of her data she found the initial categories or expected themes from her preconceptions inadequate. Within the data she uncovered richer, more salient themes then re-examined the data with these themes in view. Nawrot acknowledges the limitations of a case study focussed on just one child but at the same time shows us that in coming to know one child well, one can learn something important about all children. Finally, she describes changes in her teaching practice that resulted from her research and she identifies questions for her continuing inquiry.

In Chapter 7, Judith McIntyre offers snapshots from a two-year study of student-teacher dialogue journals from both her own classroom and those of other teachers. McIntyre sensed that something important accompanied the journal writing she undertook with her second and third grade students. She cared very much about her own classroom climate and relationships with students, and she wondered what appeared in the student-teacher journals in other classrooms. She wondered, in other words, what teachers could learn from each other's experience, and how related literature might answer questions or address concerns they had about using journals well. McIntyre's work shows student-teacher dialogue journals at their worst and best. She shows the changes that occur in another teacher's use of journals, and discusses key ideas from other researchers' work with journals. In the end, McIntyre achieves her own clarity about why the student-teacher journals are important for her.

In Chapter 8, Vireo Karvonen-Lee reports on a six-week inquiry focused on the practical problem of helping her first and second grade students learn how to paraphrase and write research reports on birds. Colleagues were an important resource for other methods to try and ways to understand the students' needs differently. The students themselves increasingly became the focus as Karvonen-Lee studied their work and used conversational interviews to understand their meanings and interpretive frameworks. She discusses what she learned about using the interview process both with colleagues and with children. She also identifies a number of teaching beliefs and assumptions she came to re-examine and revise. In her inquiry, Karvonen-Lee developed successful solutions to her practical problem. Through the reflective mode of this experience she also identified new concerns and directions for future inquiry.

In Chapter 9, Susan Hart describes her one-year experience as a teacher and researcher. Excerpts from her research journal for that year become both data and text. Her work began with a concern about hard-to-reach sixth grade students with behavioral and academic difficulties. She held a part-time teaching assignment for the year, and planned to use her non-teaching time to research. Hart provides a thorough exploration of the challenges and contradictions of being a researcher but not a teacher, or a teacher but not a researcher. In her case, the two roles merged as she became preoccupied with issues in her own teaching. Hart's work shows how researching students invariably turns teachers back to re-examining their own beliefs and practices. As she explores the contradictions in educational discourse, she concludes that teaching "the whole child" requires being a "whole teacher." She also discusses the roles of the sensory and the emotional realms in both research and teaching.

All of the inquiries discussed in this text began with individuals who took a first step into their research without being able to know in advance where the path would go or whether it would be useful. Through their self-conscious purposefulness and their openness to the data resulting from their explorations, each person's work has served to advance understanding of problems they genuinely cared about.

References

Gadamer, H-G. (1989). *Truth and Method, Second Revised Edition*. New York: Crossroad.

Greene, M. (1994). Epistemology and educational research: The influence of recent approaches to knowledge. In L. Darling-Hammond (ed.) *Review of Research in Education, Vol. 20* (pp. 423-464). Washington, DC: AERA.

Husen, T. (1988). Research paradigms in education. *Interchange, 19*(1), 2-13.

Merleau-Ponty, M. (1964). *The primacy of perception*. Evanston, IL: Northwestern University Press.

Rorty, R.M. (1982). Hermeneutics, general studies, and teaching. *Selected Papers from the Synergos Seminars, Volume 2: Hermeneutics, general studies, and teaching*, Fall 1982, 1-15.

Rorty, R. (1989). *Contingency, irony, and solidarity*. New York: Cambridge University Press.

Smith, J.K. (1993). *After the demise of empiricism: The problem of judging social and education inquiry*. CT: JAI.

Chapter Two

Interpretive Inquiry As a Formal Research Process

Julia Ellis

I ask participants in my graduate courses to undertake interpretive inquiry projects as their major assignment. To provide a mutual language for discussing the process, we use Martin Packer and Richard Addison's text, *Entering the Circle: Hermeneutic Investigations in Psychology*, and David Smith's essay, "Hermeneutic Inquiry: The Hermeneutic Imagination and the Pedagogic Text." This chapter presents the kind of discussion I offer in an introductory lecture, which draws from these sources and the work of previous students. While Hans-Georg Gadamer and other writers on hermeneutics show that the processes or dynamics of interpretation constitute our very mode of being in the world, rather than a prescribed method, students I have worked with find this presentation helpful for visualizing interpretive inquiry as a formal research process.

Central Themes in Hermeneutics
Any discussion of interpretive inquiry ought to start with a review of three themes present in hermeneutics since Schleiermacher's work in 1819. The first theme is the inherently creative character of interpretation. The interpreter works holistically, rather than (for example) using classification systems, in an effort to discern the intent or meaning behind another's expression.

The second theme, as Smith (1991) pointed out, centers on the way "good interpretation involves a playing back and forth between the specific and the general, the micro and the macro" (p. 190). Working holistically, "good interpretation

can only be pursued with a constant movement back and forth between the expression and the web of meanings within which that expression is lodged" (Smith, 1993, p. 16). To understand a part, one must understand the whole, and to understand the whole, one must understand the individual parts. One can visualize this back and forth movement between the part and the whole, a movement which has no natural starting or end point, as "'the hermeneutic circle' at work in all human understanding" (Smith, 1991, p. 190).

The third theme, already discussed in Chapter 1, is the pivotal role of language in human understanding. The language available to the interpreter both enables and limits the understanding that is possible. Since language arises from a community, reflects the influence of tradition, and marks a moment in history, history is linked with language in being understood as a condition of understanding.

Finding the Path in an Interpretive Inquiry
Students' experiences with interpretive inquiry projects nicely illustrate the expression that one "makes the path by walking it." Getting started was daunting for some course participants because they felt they lacked a definite direction or a sense of a clear destination. Was it possible that one could end up nowhere? Not knowing where one was going, might one bump into something frightening and strange? Was one really expected to travel without a map, schedule or plan? What if the project went unfinished? How could one be sure in advance that one could "do it right"? Some of the apprehension was palpable. But as early starters began sharing stories of their projects and inviting responses, more students came to appreciate the flow and unfolding quality of interpretive inquiry projects.

A Sample Study
Cory had been a secondary English teacher for three years when she learned that all ninth grade academic subjects would be assimilated for all students. She questioned whether this was a good idea given that teaching to more homogeneous ability levels seemed to her more efficient. She also worried that the less able students might lose confidence in assimilated classes.

Cory read the government rationale for this assimilation, but unconvinced by it, she undertook her own inquiry.

Cory began by interviewing small groups of students from the "basic," "general," and "advanced" classes. As expected, she learned, that like herself, the students feared that in their newly "destreamed" classes, advanced program students would be held back and basic program students would feel intimidated. She did, however, encounter a number of surprises and these new awarenesses gave direction and purpose to the remainder of her inquiries. Cory was distressed to find that basic program students already referred to themselves as "stupid" even without sharing classes with advanced program students. She was surprised that even in a differentiated curriculum, the basic program students said they wanted material that would be more helpful to them in their lives right now as many had heavy care-giving responsibilities at home. Cory was startled by the "worlds apart" life plans and expectations held by basic program students and the other students despite their young ages. She noticed that the basic program students she interviewed came from lower income life situations and wondered if this were the general trend in her school.

As her next "data collection activity," Cory checked school records to see if this socio-economic pattern was pervasive for all the ninth grade students in basic programs. She began to suspect that the parents of these students might have been less active in and confident about placement decisions at the end of eighth grade.

Next Cory looked for other research findings on the questions of concern to her and was surprised to find over 20 years of research on ability grouping and the effects of tracking. These findings and critiques often explained the phenomena she had so found remarkable in her student interviews. She also found current reports on assimilated classes and teaching models that could make them work. These models all required a letting go of the teacher-centered, single lesson, "common activity for all students" way of teaching. Instead, the teacher became a facilitator who introduced common material but then offered diverse cooperative learning activities. In ideal situations, demonstration sites helped teachers restructure their courses in these ways.

Finally, Cory interviewed the veteran teachers in her school. Her literature review suggested that long-time teachers would have dealt with ability grouping issues earlier in their careers. In the staff room, many teachers had spoken angrily against the announced assimilation. But Cory found that, one-on-one, the veteran teachers acknowledged that it would be better for the basic program students to be in "destreamed" classes. Over between 17 and 20 years of teaching they had taught their courses in both tracked and assimilated classes. Their present resistance reflected the fact that they were too tired to change how they did things yet again, and on someone else's initiative.

Cory had come full circle regarding the government rationale for assimilation. She said that at first she had understood it but not believed it. Now she believed it and had adopted it as her rationale. She also understood its implications for teachers and began lobbying articulately for the kind of support the teachers and the school would need to achieve the assimilation.

The Entry Question
Beginnings are always important and in interpretive inquiry projects one begins with an entry question. One must start with openness, humility, and genuine engagement. Cory's entry question was "Is destreaming ninth grade a good idea?" The question posed has to be a real one rather than an abstract debate or a position on an issue one wishes to promote. One must begin by acknowledging that one does not know the answer or that one does not know what to do to be helpful in a situation one cares about. Useful entry questions tend to be simple and open. They are not rhetorical; they do not imply an answer. Here are three examples:

1. *How should I work with the four "special ed" girls who now have to be mainstreamed into my fifth grade math class?*
2. *Why are the students in this junior high so hostile to teachers in the hallways?*
3. *How can I help this high school teacher who is having trouble with her math class?*

"Why is this happening?" and "How can I or anyone help?" often turn out to be the key components of entry questions. They generally reflect a relationship of care or responsibility and an attitude of openness and good will. Sometimes the questions have to do with the researcher's desire to learn from something that apparently works well. In these instances, the question often takes the form of "How does this work?" Sometimes the researcher wants to try a new procedure, idea or tool to improve or remedy things in a particular situation. In this case the question takes the form of "How might this help?"

As students search for entry questions for their interpretive inquiry projects, I encourage them to consider what preoccupies them, mystifies or confuses them, or most makes them wish that they could make a difference. Their answers to these questions are important for two reasons. First, a genuine engagement with the entry question supports the creativity and attentional energy a fruitful inquiry requires. Secondly, if one's peace is disturbed by other dilemmas, one cannot be fully attentive to the deliberation and reflection required in an interpretive inquiry project. Consequently, I am hardly surprised when students choose to focus their interpretive inquiry projects on their children or even themselves.

Notice that while the studies themselves may draw upon, create, or elaborate theory, they begin with a focus on a practical concern. The Greek word for theory, *theoria*, means behold or contemplate. In interpretive inquiry we begin with an openness to behold or contemplate life in its wholeness and complexity.

The Spiral
To track the progress or development of an interpretive inquiry project, one can find it helpful to visualize the process as a series of loops in a spiral. Each loop may represent a separate activity that resembles "data collection and interpretation." In Cory's study the four loops were interviewing students, examining demographic data in the school records, searching the literature, and interviewing teachers. Alternately, each loop may represent consecutive efforts to reinterpret one constant "text" or "set of data." I will return later to a discus-

sion of this alternative, but first I intend to discuss studies comprised of a series of explorations or "data collections" over time.

When a study is viewed as a series of loops in a spiral, each loop represents a different attempt to get closer to what one hopes to understand. One enters each loop, or separate inquiry, with a question. What one learns in the loop provides direction or a reframing of the question for the next loop. What one learns may in fact change the direction of the study quite dramatically. This happened in Cory's study when her interviews with students led her to examine school records for socio-economic patterns in tracking and subsequently, to focus her attention on her literature search. When her literature search informed her that ability grouping had been a recurring issue in education for many years, she became interested in interviewing veteran teachers about their experiences. Before I describe two other sample studies showing the series of explorations in each, I want to discuss the first loop, or the first activity one undertakes to approach what one wishes to understand.

Figure 1: Interpretive Inquiry as an Unfolding Spiral

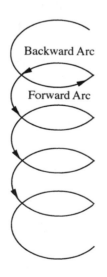

Backward Arc

Forward Arc

Each loop in the spiral represents a separate inquiry activity within the study.

Each loop may represent a separate "data collection and analysis" activity or it may represent a return to a constant set of data with, however, a different question.

Often the question for each new loop has been influenced by what was uncovered in the inquiry represented by the previous loop.

The First Loop

Once one chooses and frames an entry question, one proceeds by "doing something" to more fully encounter or access the person or situation of interest. This "doing something" (the first loop) can take a wide variety of forms, many of them apparently global or unfocused. In Cory's study, the first loop was her small-group interviewing among students from the basic, general and advanced programs. The creativity I have observed in my graduate students' first-loop choices indicates both an open entry question and a desire to respect the way their research participants might reveal themselves. Here are four examples of first activities in interpretive inquiry projects:

1. *A fifth grade teacher who wondered how to include four "special ed" girls in her very sophisticated and complex math program began by interviewing one of the girls following the interview schedule that appears in Chapter 3. In this interview, she asked no questions about math but instead worked to understand the girl better as a whole person.*

2. *A secondary school principal who supervised a second-year teacher with a difficult class for math, sat in on her class, not with his usual checklist of teaching skills but with two video cameras. Together with the teacher, he studied the video tapes to detect the dynamics at work among the students.*

3. *A teacher who had completed a diploma program in reading instruction was eager to have parents use many of her new ideas to support their children's reading growth at home. As a first inquiry, she sent parents a small pamphlet she had prepared discussing ideas for reading development. Soon after, when parents met for parent-teacher conferences, she invited their thoughts or comments about her pamphlet.*

4. *A teacher with a combined grades one, two and three class of developmentally delayed children wanted to know how well the children deal with the difficult home situa-*

tions many of them had. Since they had just completed a unit on castles, she asked them each to draw a picture of their ideal fantasy home and to indicate or label who lived there with them. When these were completed she asked each child individually to tell her about their pictures.

As my graduate students describe their interpretive inquiry projects, I observe that for two reasons the major turning point in most studies comes after the first loop. First, their understanding of the problem or question often changes dramatically. Second, the relationship they establish with the research participants changes the character of the subsequent inquiry. In the first loop of Cory's study, her concerns about justice quickly replaced her concerns about efficient teaching. When studies have such powerful first activities, they unfold in directions that few could have predicted. When researchers present weaker first activities, they often feel stuck after the first loop and unsure where to go next. This pattern leads to the idea of "uncovering."

Uncovering
Each loop or exploration, which can be understood as data collection and interpretation, generates findings. Some of these findings may well be what the researcher expected. Others, however, may be surprises. Cory found that the students shared her fear that basic program students would be intimidated in assimilated classes. This she expected. But she also encountered surprises about the meaning and effects of tracked classes for basic program students. In hermeneutic terms, these unexpected dimensions are called *uncoverings*. While uncoverings may not lead directly to a solution, they often enable a researcher to understand the problem or question differently and so to reframe it usefully for planning the next step in the inquiry. The uncoverings from Cory's student interviews prompted her to examine demographic data in school records and gave her focus and purpose as she studied the related literature.

This idea of uncovering, developed by Heidegger in *Being and Time* (1927/1962, p. 56, cited by Packer and Addison, 1989, p. 278) is important to interpretive inquiry. Packer and

Addison (1989) noted that the Greek word for "truth," *aletheia* can be translated as unconcealed, unhidden or uncovered. If some aspect of a person or situation has eluded our awareness, our research works to "let it show itself, not forcing our perspective on it. And we must do this in a way that respects the way it shows itself" (p. 278). The uncovering is the return arc of the hermeneutic circle and the response to our inquiry. Thus, if no surprises occur, we either do not yet "see" what can be uncovered, or we have not yet approached the research participant or situation in a way that respects the way it can show itself. It became a matter of some amusement and anxiety in our courses to recognize that if one encountered no surprises, the research had stalled.

Two Sample Studies
Two more studies illustrate the conversational orientation interpretive inquiry can take. Both studies have easily discernible separate loops in the spiral of the interpretive inquiry. You can see examples of questions reframed when one uncovering leads to the next step in the inquiry. You can also see a variety of approaches used to allow research participants to show themselves.

EXAMPLE ONE—TEENAGER/ADULT RELATIONSHIPS: Mary taught health and science in a junior high school. While her interactions with students in class were agreeable, she felt confused by the change in the students' behavior in the hallways. They would never greet or even acknowledge her as she passed their way. They appeared withdrawn from and hostile toward all adults. In this map or outline of Mary's inquiry I use italics to emphasize the connections or linkages between one inquiry activity and the next.

As the first activity in her research, Mary asked a small group of students to help her preview a film for possible use in health class. As she listened to their discussion of the film she heard their *general grief about their location in life as teenagers.*

As the next loop in the spiral of her inquiry, she asked two classes to complete a brief questionnaire inviting completion of such statements as *"Being a teenager is. . . ,"* and "I am happiest when. . . ." Mary identified *recurring themes*, expressions, and complaints in the questionnaire responses, and as the third loop, she *brought these back to the classes for discussion* and elaboration. Listening to the students talk, she heard their discouragement with the *futility of interactions with adults*. They felt extremely frustrated in their communication and negotiation with adults, especially their parents.

As the fourth loop, Mary approached *resource people and the literature to search for ideas* about ways to help the students with their trouble. She found a program package that introduced students to the notion of communication in the role of "child," "parent," and "adult." The package had many role plays for students to practice. Mary began using the package in her classes and some students promptly reported on their efforts with their new awareness at home.

EXAMPLE TWO—THE NEW NURSE: As part of her hospital management duties, Janet was responsible for the nursing staff in an intermediate care unit. Jim, a recently graduated male nurse, had been part of the staff for several weeks when many of the nurses began to complain about being assigned to work with him. None of them offered any specific reasons why or specified anything in particular he had done wrong.

As the first step in her inquiry, Janet followed routine procedures by conducting a standardized interview with Jim to assess his general knowledge. Having determined his general knowledge to be satisfactory, she still had no way to understand the discomfort of the other nurses.

As her second inquiry activity, Janet conducted a simulation exercise with Jim in an empty hospital room, describing the conditions of imaginary patients in beds A, B, C and D. At a certain point in the simulation, she told Jim that patient B was starting to have an emergency and she asked him what he would do. He said that he would sit and talk with patient A, who was depressed. When Janet expressed surprise, he explained that all of the other nurses would unfailingly attend to an emergency but they never took time for the patient who was depressed. In the course of a lengthy follow-up discussion, Janet determined that Jim had a strong desire to continue working in an intermediate care unit rather than a different ward, and Jim acknowledged that it was understandable that other nurses wouldn't feel comfortable working with someone whose response to an emergency was unpredictable.

As the final loop of her inquiry, Janet observed the work of a team of nurses with Jim as a member of the team, and she noticed two patterns. First none of the nurses were mentoring Jim. Nobody was saying, "Here, you try it this time." Second, she "saw" for the first time that nothing about his appearance or persona invited mentoring. He looked strong, had held an administrative position in a previous career, and carried himself with authority. Janet later advised the nurses that they would have to make a conscious effort to start mentoring Jim as a new graduate and staff member.

In each of her inquiries, Janet attempted to understand how Jim experienced being a nurse in their ward and how other nurses experienced working with him. Ideas for inquiry activities come from knowing the context and the opportunities for inquiry the context affords.

Both of these studies show interpretive inquiry as part of an on-going conversation. Even with their written accounts completed, Mary remained in her school and continued to help her students. Janet and Jim and the other nurses continued to find ways to work together. Both Mary and Janet collected only as much "data" in their explorations as they could manageably study, learn from, and act upon. Within the constraints of the available time and energy, they had both taken a variety of approaches to enable their research participants to "show themselves." The strategies they used illustrate practicably how a fusion of horizons can be accomplished through a dialogue of questions and answers with the research participant or "text." In both of these examples, the researchers' discoveries and expanded understandings enabled them to identify promising directions for helpful action. Solution strategies are often well within our repertoires; it is mainly our understanding of the problem that requires growth.

Single-loop Studies
In the two examples of interpretive inquiries just described, the researchers had little difficulty "seeing" what they had uncovered. But it is not always this easy. In these "multi-loop"

studies, the researchers had a variety of opportunities for conversations with their research participants. Some studies look more like a single loop in that only one "data collection" activity occurs or the "data" for the study already exist in some sort of textual form.

In these instances, a researcher often makes repeated loops with the same data set, re-examining the data each time with a question reframed from what emerged from the previous set of deliberations. In studies of this form, the researcher's experience of the forward and backward arcs of the hermeneutic circle becomes even more pronounced.

Theses often combine "multi-loop" and "single-loop" inquiries. When a study entails a series of interviews and observations, what the researcher learns in each activity provides a focus or reframed question for the next inquiry. At the end of the data collection, the researcher then works again with all transcripts, field notes, research notes, and artifacts, experiencing them as a whole or single text. Although the researcher has been making sense of these data all along, the task at the end is to articulate the most coherent and comprehensive account of what one can learn from the sum of the inquiries. Each transcript and field note has become part of a whole and the meaning of each can now be reconsidered in relation to the whole. I present an example of a brief single-loop study immediately after the following discussion of the forward and backward arc of the hermeneutic circle.

The Forward and Backward Arc
Packer and Addison (1989) explained that in the forward arc of the hermeneutic circle, projection, one uses "fore-structure" to make some initial sense of the research participant, text or data. That is, one uses one's existing preconceptions, pre-understandings or prejudices—including purposes, interests, and values—to interpret; this initial approach is unavoidable. But in the backward arc, one evaluates the initial interpretation and attempts to see what went unseen before. In this evaluation process, one reconsiders the interpretation by re-examining the data for confirmation, contradictions, gaps or inconsistencies. This re-examination may require charts or summaries or lists in order to uncover patterns or relationships

difficult to discern when one considers a large amount of information simultaneously. In this process it is just as important to ask what is absent in the data as what is present. Re-examining the data is a deliberative process. In the effort to see what was previously invisible, one's question must be genuine and one must search for the coherence and reasonableness in the behavior of others.

A researcher does not seek a uniquely correct or "accurate" interpretation, but rather the most adequate one that can be developed at that time. In this search, the researcher will often explore the interpretive power of other conceptual frameworks. The search is for an interpretation as coherent, comprehensive, and comprehensible as possible.

Figure 2: The Hermeneutic Circle

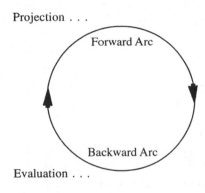

Projection . . . entails making sense of a research participant, situation, or a set of data by drawing on one's forestructure, which is the current product of one's autobiography (beliefs, values, interests, interpretive frameworks) and one's relationship to the question or problem (pre-understandings and concerned engagement).

Evaluation . . . entails endeavoring to see what went unseen in the initial interpretation resulting from projection. The data are re-examined for contradictions, gaps, omissions, or confirmations of the initial interpretation. Alternate interpretive frameworks are purposefully searched for and "tried on."

An Example of a Single-loop Study
One would be hard-pressed to find a drama book Ann had not read or a drama course she had not taken or taught. She taught drama in a secondary school and she wanted to use her graduate-level interpretive inquiry project to advance her understanding of her own teaching there. The drama department in her school required her to give a departmental exam, and so she asked her twelfth grade drama students to write a paper about the benefits they had derived from their drama course.

Ann decided that instead of just marking her students' papers she would study them for her interpretive inquiry project. For a long time, Ann found herself stalled in the backward arc. It was hard for her to see anything she had not already seen. For every benefit the students reported, Ann could cite the page, author, and title of a book she had read that already described these benefits. Ann's graduate colleagues were sympathetic. Ann knew so much about drama. What could she possibly learn from her students?

Finally, Ann's deliberations led her to see something she had not noticed before. A certain pattern intrigued her. The students who reported the greatest number of benefits were also the students who were the most open about themselves in general. Ann had frequently used debriefing discussions after the activities or exercises in her drama class, and she recognized that the students who were the least open in their papers (and who also claimed the fewest number of benefits from drama) had also been the least active participants in the oral debriefing sessions in class. Since senior drama was an elective course, Ann could safely conclude that they all wanted to be there, and she planned to pursue the reflection aspect of her drama course with greater attention the following year.

Ann's study exemplifies the generativity of interpretive inquiry. The study opened up a new question and focus for inquiry about her drama teaching. She found a promising starting point for enriching her classroom. Ann's experience with the interpretive inquiry process also shows how difficult it can be to move beyond one's usual categories to see what one has previously missed. One has to believe that patterns or relationships remain to be discovered, andnd one has to search for the coherence and reasonableness in the behavior of others.

Evaluating an Interpretive Account
Ann's research demonstrates the kinds of outcomes one can expect from an interpretive inquiry. Packer and Addison (1989) have suggested these possible outcomes:

1. *Ideas for helpful action are identified.*

2. *New questions or concerns come to the researcher's attention.*

3. *The researcher is changed by the research—that is, the researcher discovers inadequacies in his or her own initial pre-understandings.*

In evaluating an interpretive account, Packer and Addison emphasized that validity is not the issue in terms of proving an interpretation true or false. "Validation" would imply the possibility of interpretation-free norms or standards. Instead, the question is whether the interpretive account can be clarified or made more comprehensive and comprehensible.

Concerns about "validity" stem from the fear that without validation procedures interpretive accounts might be viewed as mere opinion or speculation. The impulse towards the grammar of validation originated in the natural sciences paradigm where hypotheses were treated as guesses to be tested. An interpretive account is neither a guess nor a speculation. It is instead "the working out of possibilities that have become apparent in a preliminary, dim understanding of events" (Packer and Addison, 1989, p. 277). The fore-structure or pre-understanding of the researcher who has entered the circle with humility and inquisitiveness will include a kind of caring concern that accommodates a perspective or way of reading which might otherwise be impossible to achieve. Thus, the interpretation is ordered and organized by the fore-structure and further guided by "a sense of the complexity of the human relationship between researcher and research participant" (Packer and Addison, 1989, p. 277). In other words, the concerned engagement researchers bring to the question and the human solidarity they seek through the inquiry give direction and guidance to their interpretations.

Some may at first view the hermeneutic circle as tautological in that one can only understand in terms of what one already knows. Packer and Addison suggest, however, that a circularity of understanding is essential and that the real test of an inquiry or interpretation is whether or not it reveals a solution to the difficulty that motivated the inquiry. They suggest that a "true interpretive account" helps researchers, and the people they study, and ultimately supports progress with addressing their concerns. They note that "concerned engagement" distinguishes interpretive inquiry from those other forms of human inquiry that seek only to describe or just to understand human phenomena.

Thus, when we evaluate an interpretive account, we try less to determine whether it has provided validated knowledge or timeless truth than to ask whether our concern has been advanced. Packer and Addison reviewed the four general approaches to evaluating interpretive accounts: (1)requiring that it be coherent; (2)examining its relationship to external evidence; (3)seeking consensus among various groups; and (4)assessing its relationship to future events. While these approaches may not make interpretation-free validation possible, they are reasonable approaches to use in that they direct attention and discussion to considerations researchers value when asking whether "what has been uncovered in an interpretive inquiry answers the practical, concernful question that directed that inquiry" (p. 289). They also caution, however, that any one of the four approaches may fail to support an interpretation and that, in fact, sometimes none of them will, as when an interpretation that brings a solution to a practical problem may at first seem implausible and unconnected.

In summary, one should avoid confusing an evaluation of an interpretive account with the sort of objective validation traditional approaches seek. To evaluate an account, one should ask whether the concern which motivated the inquiry has been advanced. To judge whether an answer has been uncovered by an interpretive account, use the following six questions to direct attention to considerations we value:

1. *Is it plausible, convincing?*

2. *Does it fit with other material we know?*

3. *Does it have the power to change practice?*

4. *Has the researcher's understanding been transformed?*

5. *Has a solution been uncovered?*

6. *Have new possibilities been opened up for the researcher, research participants, and the structure of the context?*

Writing the Interpretive Account
Each research story is different and invites a different reportorial mode. Moreover, each time one tells the story, one may tell it from a changed perspective. When my students write interpretive accounts as course assignments, I encourage them to begin as though writing in a journal, starting with how they came to be concerned for, interested in, or knowledgeable about their entry question. If they have already studied literature pertinent to their question, I invite them either to present some of the key ideas or theories that influence their thinking or simply to interweave these ideas conversationally where it informs their consideration of findings. Just as I encourage them to mention the theoretical literature that informs their interpretations, I also encourage them to relate autobiographical material that predisposes their responses to or interpretations of people, events, or texts. This practice encourages a self-consciousness about their fore-structures and helps them to become aware of their taken-for-granted assumptions about the way life is or should be.

When my students enjoy ample time, as when working on a thesis rather than a course assignment, I encourage them to begin their writing with a personal story that can help us all understand their concerned engagement with their question. I remember one lengthy conference with a graduate student concerned about the way many boys give up "the fun" of ice hockey at the age of ten or eleven. At the end of our meeting we stood chatting in the hallway where he told me about going home to Ottawa for Christmas and how much he looked forward to skating down the Rideau River with his friends. They would take their hockey sticks and pass a puck back and forth because that just made it "more fun." Then he told me childhood stories about being the first one out of the classroom at the end of each day to run home, finish his homework, race to the neighborhood rink, plough off any new snow, and play hockey in sub-zero weather. Until he told me these stories, I had not really understood what he meant by "fun" in his thesis or why he was so concerned about ten-year-olds putting their skates away.

The personal story at the beginning of an interpretive account can powerfully support a reader's fusion of horizons with the text. The personal story provides access to the writer's perspective and the meanings that words and events hold for him or her. Creating an opportunity for more shared meanings at the beginning of the text can certainly make the interpretive account more comprehensible.

Regardless of the format, components, or sequence of the interpretive account, it must function as a well-argued essay. One way or another, the writers offer interpretations or arguments and they must support them by enough illustrative material to enable readers with different perspectives to form their own interpretations. The readers should have enough illustrative material to make sense of the research from their own standpoints while still understanding how the researcher could see things the way that he or she does.

Finally, a particular signature of interpretive inquiry is self-conscious reflection. Writers often make a point of identifying those places in their studies where they became aware of the inadequacies of their pre-understandings. Sometimes they report these points as a part of the movement of the study. Sometimes they include a special reflection section where they examine how the research has transformed their understanding. Wherever it occurs, this reflection is the thread that holds the research story together.

References

Packer, M.J., & Addison, R.B. (Eds.) (1989). *Entering the circle: Hermeneutic investigation in psychology.* Albany: SUNY Press.

Smith, D.G. (1991). Hermeneutic inquiry: The hermeneutic imagination and the pedagogic text. In E.C. Short (ed.), *Forms of curriculum inquiry* (pp. 187-210). Albany: SUNY Press.

Smith, J.K. (1993). *After the demise of empiricism: The problem of judging social and educational inquiry.* CT: JAI.

Chapter Three _____

Narrative Inquiries with Children and Youth

Julia Ellis

An Introduction to Narrative Inquiry
Recently, I found myself working with a small group of
student teachers completing a three-month practicum at an
elementary school. One of the student teachers, Karen, was
having difficulty with John, a fifth grade student in her math
and social studies classes. John persisted in calling out whenever he wished to speak, which made things awkward for
Karen. She described John as very bright but said that he
failed to respond to her requests that he raise his hand. Finally
the school principal advised Karen to set up a behavior
contract for John. I had Karen ask the principal to wait two
days while she tried something else first. I brought Karen the
interview schedule included as Appendix A to this chapter and
she used it to initiate a narrative inquiry with the boy. After
she finished her interview with John, she got into her car and
drove home. While driving, she thought about what he had
said and his behavior became much more understandable, and
once his behavior made more sense, she knew what to do to
help.
     In the interview, John had told Karen how he experienced
discussions at home with his parents and older brother. He
never got to speak because they always told him to wait, but
their conversations just moved along and they never let him
in. He also revealed his disappointment that while his older
brother had made the hockey team and had received ex-
pensive new equipment, he had not been selected for a team.
     The next day, Karen took two new approaches to John.
Whenever he did raise his hand, she called on him right away.
This was, she felt, the appropriate way for him to see and trust

that hand raising would earn him his turn to speak. Also, since she was in charge of intra-murals for the three-month practicum, she appointed him captain of intra-mural sports for his class. He was thrilled.

The story of Karen's response to John shows narrative inquiry serving as a form of interpretive inquiry when it begins from concerned engagement. Karen had a practical question and a genuine caring embodied in her pre-understanding—all of which gave her attention and sense-making direction as she considered the significance of the stories John told her. Her openness and good will made possible a reading of John's stories that led first to uncoverings then to ideas for helpful action.

In such other modes of human inquiry as sociology and anthropology, researchers often use narrative inquiry less to grasp the uniqueness of the individuals studied, than to understand their lives as examples of larger social phenomena. For example, in reporting on her narrative study of women superintendents' experiences, Susan Chase (1996) explained that while in the process of conducting an interview, the narrator and listener share the goal of hearing and understanding the unfolding story in full detail. Thereafter, however, their interests diverge. Chase's narrators had been interested in describing and explaining their experiences. In narrative analysis, however, Chase was interested in analyzing the cultural processes such stories take for granted rather than the content of the stories themselves. Therefore, in her analyses, her interpretation focused on the set of language processes characteristic of everyday speech. She sought to show how language constraints, even more than structural constraints, shape professional women's lives in invisible, taken-for-granted ways.

When one adopts narrative inquiry in order to understand broad social phenomena more clearly, one rarely expects to intervene in the lives of the people studied. Instead, one elicits and interprets stories in order to understand how some aspect of our world works. Narrative inquiry displays some elements of *interpretive inquiry* in psychology therapy relationships. Therapists who work more holistically with stories, rather than simply imposing interpretations from authorized theories and definitions, seek to understand a person's behavior and ideas

from their stories (Sarbin, 1986). Robert Coles, notably, emphasized an awareness of "patients as storytellers" in his
1989 book, *The Call of Stories.*

The identification of narrative inquiry with psychology
and psychiatry sometimes makes student teachers apprehensive about their work with this exalted and esoteric mode of
inquiry. For six years, I assigned student teachers to undertake
a narrative inquiry with a student in their practicum school
(Ellis, 1992, 1994). In the first years, some student teachers
expressed concern that they lacked the psychology background to allow them to formulate interpretations of any
students they might interview. Thus, as a prelude to this assignment, I began to offer my classes more background in hermeneutics and narrative inquiry.

When we recognize that interpretive inquiry describes our
very mode of being in the world, we then realize that we
respond to people on the basis of how we have already
"read" or "interpreted" them. When we intentionally undertake narrative inquiry we give ourselves the chance to develop
our understanding of the other person beyond what it was and
perhaps to correct our "misreadings." Conducting a narrative
inquiry, we take conscious responsibility for our interpretation
of the other person. During the interview process, we establish
a bond or solidarity with the other. From what we come to see,
we can imagine how to be more practically helpful, and importantly for our students, the more fully we understand them, the
more fully they can experience themselves as their self-
understanding passes through the screen of our interpretation.

Narrative inquiry comes naturally with friends or loved
ones as we listen to and consider the significance of their
stories. The process is continual and the interpretations are
seldom final ones. Thus, when we take up a narrative inquiry
with students in the way this chapter outlines, we make a
concerted effort to understand them as we would understand
any other friend.

This chapter describes the narrative inquiry activity my
students and I have developed. I learned a great deal from
studying my students' inquiries. Initially, the instructions I
offered them were vague; in the first year, only a few students
produced strong work. I studied how they had proceeded and

incorporated the resultant ideas into my subsequent instructions. Thereafter, all but a few students completed strong and
exciting work with their narrative inquiries.

The Narrative Inquiry Activity

At first glance, the narrative inquiry activity may appear to be
cumbersome, time-consuming, and even irrelevant to the work
of learning to teach. The activity entails a one-hour interview
with a student, transcribing the audio tape of the interview,
composing a narrative portrait, and writing reflections. Some
students complained about the amount of time all this work
required. Once they had finished, however, many reported to
me or their advisors that it was the most worthwhile assignment
they had completed in their entire graduate program. Each
year, more students responded enthusiastically to the idea of
the activity, welcoming its real-life, hands-on, non-abstract
quality. I worked with students specializing in both secondary
and elementary education—the majority, however, in elementary education. In the following sections I briefly discuss
the preparation for the interview, the interview questions, the
interview process, writing the narrative portrait, writing the
reflections, and presenting the follow-up discussions. In a
concluding section, I review theoretical issues pertaining to
narrative accounts and identity.

Preparing for the Interview

Choosing and inviting a student to participate in a narrative
inquiry may be the most interesting part of the preparation.
Student teachers are pleased when they are permitted to invite
a student of their choice rather than simply accepting the
cooperating teacher's selection. Sometimes student teachers
find they choose students much like themselves at the same
age. Some student teachers intentionally choose students they
find mysterious or interesting because of their differences.
Some puposefully select the "class clown," "rebel," or "ring
leader." I never suggest that my student teachers select
students who obviously have difficulties. I simply invite them
to choose someone they think they will be comfortable with
and interested in interviewing. I also recommend the age of
ten as a minimum for interviewees although many working in

fourth grade classrooms choose nine-year-olds. Student teachers working in primary grades visit older classes and then interview a student from that group. I include a sample consent letter for parents as Appendix B.

Three other parts of the practical preparation for the interview follow. First, find a quiet, private location for the interview and visit it with the student before the interview itself. Second, transpose the interview questions to file cards, with one question per card, and fasten the cards with binder rings. With one question per card, the interviewers need not worry about losing their place in the interview schedule while following up responses to a question. Also, interviewees cannot read the questions upside down if they are on separate sheets. Third, some student teachers complete a practice interview with a young friend or relative. Listening to a tape recording of the practice interview helps them notice aspects of their interviewing styles they may wish to modify.

The Interview Questions
The interview questions developed from my thesis work (Ellis, 1983), in which I compiled case studies of the everyday behavior of creative fifth grade children. When I later taught an adolescent psychology course, some of the students in that course used the questions to guide case studies of adolescents they knew. Their response to the questions was so positive that I began to offer the narrative inquiry activity as an assignment in other courses. The interview questions appear to work by evoking a variety of memories, feelings, and categories of activity interviewees like to report. A particular strength of the questions is their open-endedness. They avoid eliciting specific factual information. Instead, they invite interviewees to search for memories or thoughts they would like to talk about.

Some student teachers have raised three concerns about the interview questions. First, considering the questions literally from an adult perspective, some thought they themselves would want a whole week to answer some of them. They placed such questions as "What's the most difficult thing you've ever had to do?" in that category. In the interview process itself, however, the question tends to function more as though it were worded, "Tell me a story about something that was difficult to do." The question either evokes a memory or not. In all of the transcripts I have examined, children either reply with a story or they say, "I can't think of anything." None of them ever said, "I can't decide." All of the questions are simply prompts to help children think of topics that may be salient for them. Some questions work well this way and some do not, but it is difficult to make predictions about responses to any of the questions.

Second, student teachers worry that children may offer different responses to questions on different occasions. It is certainly reasonable to expect that this will, in fact, occur. If, however, a child has a major preoccupation or organizing frame of reference, it will probably manifest itself one way or another on different occasions. (Such major preoccupations show themselves when, for example, a child answers the large majority of the questions by relating answers to a single topic or theme like a favourite sport, a chronic disease, or an inclination to be competitive and to perceive others as intensely competitive.) If no generalized, pervasive preoccupation emerges, a researcher can infer that the child is offering a collection of stories from his or her bank of stories. Because the form provides 26 questions or invitations for stories, those stories—whichever a student may recite on any particular day—will tap into the interests, pastimes, hopes, fears, likes, antagonisms, and experiences that are part of the child's reality. A child's answer to any one question will not determine the interviewer's interpretation of that child; rather, the interviewer will consider the collection of stories and the connections among them to arrive at a more complete sense of the child as a whole person.

Third, student teachers express concern that it may be bad form to pose questions with words the child may not understand. But as I have discussed elsewhere (Ellis, 1994), the shared search for a common referent for language is part of the process of creating solidarity in the interview process. Student teachers often find this the case with, for example, the question about "willpower." When children ask what willpower is, student teachers usually enjoy giving examples from their own lives of how or when they had to use it.

The Interview Process

The interview that follows the interview schedule provided at the end of this chapter presents an ideal "getting-to-know-you" opportunity. At the beginning, however, both interviewer and interviewee may feel a bit apprehensive. The interviewer may be afraid the child will have nothing to say. The child may be uncertain about the kinds of answers that will gain the interviewer's acceptance and approval. During the course of the school day, we mainly listen to students when they bring in stories from recess or the weekend. This kind of talk feels comfortable and familiar. It is easy to receive enthusiastic stories. But in the interview we invite the child's reflections, dreams, hopes, fears, and sense-making. We have to listen hard, focus and concentrate in order to frame follow-up questions that show our genuine interest.

The sight of the tape recorder may cause some children anxiety. It often works well to have the child speak into it, then play back the voice to "test" the machine before starting the interview. The interviewer can place the machine close to the child with the understanding that he or she can turn it off at any time during the interview. Guidelines for conducting the interview appear in Appendix C.

Most children clearly enjoy the attention of the interview. After they have heard and responded to the first few questions they visibly relax, showing that they have the feel of how the interview works. The interviewer's responses to the child's first few responses are, however, crucial. It is important to communicate acceptance and interest without expressing so much enthusiasm that the child thinks that those are the only kinds of answers to offer. It helps if an interviewer can avoid evaluative responses like "That's a good answer!" or "Good!" It also helps to reassure children if they say "I don't know" and can't think of an answer to a question. Let them know that not all of the questions "work well" and that you will try another question to see if that one sparks a memory of something enjoyable to talk about. At the end of an interview, be sure to ask children if they have any questions they want to ask.

Throughout the interview it is important to communicate acceptance and genuine interest. One must honestly believe that the child's thoughts and feelings are reasonable and use follow-up questions to ascertain why they make sense. A mother practicing the interview questions with her nine-year-old son was shocked and disappointed at the cartoon character he said was his hero. She wanted to respond by saying it was a poor choice but caught herself and followed up with, "And why is he your hero?" She was surprised that her son's explanation made good sense. While showing interest and acceptance with follow-up questions, the interviewer must also convey an impression of relaxed conversation with no need to rush or say everything in one day.

Offering girls a safe place for their self-presentation can involve extra consideration. Young girls generally have already internalized the societal expectation to present themselves modestly and as fitting stereotypes. The interviewer may need to communicate a great deal of respect, openness and positive expectation for girls like these to feel free to present their achievements, aspirations, and atypical interests or experiences.

Some student teachers ask whether they should split the interview questions over two sessions. Almost all of them complete the interview in one session, but a few find it becoming tiresome for the child and consider two sessions preferable. If the child gives long answers or finds the reflection the questions invite strenuous, it may be useful to have anticipated a place in the interview schedule to close a first session.

The process of the interview itself creates or deepens the relationship or bond between interviewer and interviewee. As a post-interview practice, it is important to keep this established bond in mind and make a point to acknowledge the child with a friendly comment the first time you see him or her again in the classroom or another context. The child will be looking for this recognition of the special importance of the conversation you shared. If, in the interview, the child discloses difficult life events, one can occasionally ask how things are going in a way that communicates your confidence in the child's ability to cope with life as she or he finds it.

Writing the Narrative Portrait

The narrative portrait requires deliberative writing. It presents an opportunity to make connections and develop insights from patterns and relationships one finds among the child's collection of stories and ideas. It can be helpful to begin the analysis by clustering the stories or statements according to such recurring topics as friends, sports, family, school work, or interests. One can then look across the clusters of stories attempting to discern values, concerns, predispositions, ways of proceeding, or ways of making sense of social situations that reappear across clusters of stories. Such values, preoccupations, or interpretive frameworks can be pulled out to form their own "clusters" as well.

It can also be useful to write a first paragraph that serves as a sketch incorporating the most prominent or interesting aspects of the child as a person. The rest of the portrait can then develop each of these "themes" or "arguments" more thoroughly. The narrative portrait, like any well-argued essay, should provide ample illustrative material to support or clarify any descriptions or interpretations.

At the point in one's analysis where the stories have just been clustered, one can ask what each cluster of stories is about at a thematic rather than a topical level. For example, are all of the stories about sports connected by the theme of competition, or of fun, or of interaction with friends and family? During this search, one hopes to grasp the meaning and significance of the topic for the child. One may find themes connecting a number of topics in ways that reveal a child's dominant characteristics, motivations, values, interests or preoccupations. Themes can be thought of as "knots in the webs of our experience, around which certain experiences are spun and thus experienced as meaningful wholes" (van Manen, 1984, p. 59).

After working with the clusters of stories and statements in the ways just discussed, one can usefully ask a number of other questions about the clusters of stories. What is absent in these stories: friends, places (other than home and school), talk of the past, talk of the future, hope? When significant others appear in the stories, who are they and how does the child position himself or herself in relation to them? Is there a balance in the time frames across stories or are they positioned mainly in the past or future? Does the child incorporate past experiences into a present identity and a hopeful story for the future? Does the child use a particular metaphor as a key interpretive device for making sense of events or solving problems? Is the child passive or active in the majority of stories? Does the child's talk reveal a "beyond-her-years" interpretive scheme appropriated or learned from family or community? I am reminded here of a student teacher who, after interviewing a ten-year-old girl in his practicum class and thereby learning her political views, said he better appreciated that many in his class of ten-year-olds might have the ideas of forty-year-olds.

These analyses can help one write a portrait in which one organizes an understanding of the child's understanding of reality. What results is not a chronological life history but a portrayal of what engages, preoccupies, motivates, pleases, interests, frightens or displeases this person. Talents, skills, abilities, and life experiences may also be revealed. As well, one may articulate a sense of how the child makes sense of himself and others. As we understand a child's story in this way, we can anticipate the opportunities for congruence or reciprocity between the child's story and the classroom story we support for children. As we better understand what is already motivating a child, we can consider how classroom routines and and instructional activities and content can be modified to to work well with a child's interests and aspirations.

Writing Reflections on the Narrative Portrait
In writing a narrative portrait, we acknowledge that stories mean more than they can say. The deliberation inherent in crafting the narrative portrait represents a search for meaning in the stories and statements offered during the interview. When writing reflections on the narrative inquiry, a researcher searches for the personal significance of that experience. Through this writing, the interviewer formulates and sets down the insights, awarenesses, convictions, and ideas the inquiry made possible.

To help them write their reflections, I ask my student teachers to express what they have learned from the experience about the particular child, about children in general, about themselves, and about teaching. A list of questions that prompt these reflections appears in Appendix D. The active search for the meaning and significance of the narrative inquiry can be remarkably productive. While many student teachers at first consider this exercise redundant, they are always surprised at the awarenesses and implications they identify as they write. Searching reflectively for the implications of what they have discovered, learned, or experienced, they come away changed by the research and find personal meaning in the narrative inquiry experience.

Follow-up Discussions and Sharing

After my student teachers complete their written reports on the narrative inquiry, I reserve two in-class activities for follow-up discussions. As the first activity, student teachers exchange written reports with a partner, read each other's work, then discuss their thoughts and questions. Many of them bring their issues and questions forward for general discussion. The student teachers usually find that reading someone else's report helps them appreciate more the student they worked with themselves.

In the second activity, student teachers identify a distinguishing characteristic of the student they interviewed and then form discussion groups according to these characteristics. Examples of distinguishing characteristics include being a high achiever, being strongly sports oriented, being the class clown, being a child of immigrants, and so forth. If no such characteristic emerges, we use the gender and grade level of the student as a category for forming discussion groups. In these small groups, the student teachers seek to identify and discuss what was common to the students they had interviewed, what surprised or puzzled them about these students, and the teaching practices they expect to be helpful to such students. Each group reports their findings and ideas to the whole class.

Interviewing Parents

In completing a narrative inquiry with a child, it can be helpful to add an interview with the parents. In my initial work with narrative inquiry (Ellis, 1983), I folllowed the schedule in

Appendix E as I interviewed parents. The anecdotes and observations obtained from the parent interview can be integrated
with those obtained from the child when forming clusters of
stories as part of the preparation and analysis involved in
crafting a narrative portrait. Parent interviews that follow this
schedule range from 45 to 90 minutes.

The Nature of Self-narratives

This chapter presented narrative inquiry as a form of interpretive inquiry designed to increase an understanding that can
inform helpful action. It has methodologically described the
narrative inquiry with children and youth undertaken by a
large number of student teachers I have worked with. This
concluding section outlines some generally held understandings about the nature of narrative accounts which people
offer about their experiences. These ideas have implications
for questions about the verifiability or completeness of narrative accounts, the possibility of a "true" or autonomous
identity, and the reasons for undertaking narrative inquiry
with children or youth.

The narrative accounts people generate should be understood, not as records of what happened but as current drafts of
their own interpretive search for cause-and-effect or connections among self-relevant events. This reflective work is on-
going as, throughout their lives, people search for coherence,
historical unity, and meaningful integration of their experiences (Carr, 1986; Polkinghorne, 1988). As new events
unfold, people often revise their interpretations of the
meaning or significance of prior events. As we saw in Chapter
1, the perceptions or interpretations a person can achieve at
any given time are both encouraged and limited by language,
social context, and history. We are born into the stories we
hear about the way the world works. Narrators can use only
the language available to them to explain their experiences.
Thus, as Polkinghorne (1988) observed, language is not a
"transparent tool" that reflects reality but a "distorting
screen" that projects experience onto the interpretation of
reality (p. 26). Discourse analysts (Florio-Ruane 1991; Potter
and Wetherell, 1987; Wetherell and Potter, 1988) have also
noted that people may present narrative accounts differently

on different occasions according to the functions they intend their accounts to serve. Bruner (1990), too, has emphasized that narrative accounts are neither right nor wrong but represent efforts to mediate culture and the individual's "more idiosyncratic world of beliefs, desires, and hopes" (p. 87).

To be intelligible to others, a narrator's language and story structure must be congruent with cultural expectations about how life experiences can be structured. Thus Gergen and Gergen (1987) argued that self-narratives are "preeminently social" and reflect a means by which to carry out relationships with others rather than enduring psychological dispositions. The need to be understood by others thus supports a certain "communal organization of self-experience" (Potter and Wetherell, 1987, p. 106, as cited in Bowman, 1996, p. 55).

Many conclude that the search for a person's true self-identity is futile given that people are multidimensional, are always at work at reinterpreting their experiences, appropriate communally shared frameworks for interpreting those experiences, and tell stories in ways that serve different purposes on different occasions. But no one denies the role of social obligations or commitments in supporting a sense of self or identity. In his book *After Virtue*, MacIntyre argued that moral action is that action which maintains the continuity of one's story in terms of one's role or relationship as sister, parent, teacher, and so forth. Harre and Gillett (1994) described the self as depending on the sense of place an individual has, not only physically, but also socially in terms of mutual obligations and commitments. Bettelheim (1994) discussed "belonging" and "having a rightful place" as depending upon being needed and contributing to the survival or welfare of the family or community. In his analysis of current culture he suggested how difficult it can be for children to experience a "rightful place."

At this time, perhaps more than any other before, it is crucial that we hear children's stories and listen for the ways in which they try to secure rightful places. While these places cannot be "granted" but can only be secured through the children's own efforts, the understanding and thoughtful teacher can recognize and support those efforts, as Karen did with John in the story that began this chapter.

References

Bettelheim, B. (1994). Seeking a rightful place. *The NAMTA Journal, 19*(2), 101-118.

Boman, J. (1996). Effective use of humor in nursing practice: Analyzing the discourse of nurses known for making it happen. Unpublished doctoral dissertation, University of Alberta.

Bruner, J. (1990). *Acts of meaning*. Cambridge, MA: Harvard University Press.

Carr, D. (1986). *Time, narrative and history*. Bloomington: Indiana University Press.

Chase, S. (1996). Personal vulnerability and interpretive authority in narrative research. In R. Josselson (ed.), *Ethics and process in the narrative study of lives* (pp. 45-59). Thousand Oaks, CA: Sage Publications.

Coles, R. (1989). *The call of stories: Teaching and the moral imagination*. Boston: Houghton Mifflin Company.

Ellis, J. (1983). Development of a new measure of creative abilites in grade five children. Unpublished doctoral dissertation, University of British Columbia.

Ellis, J. L. (1992). Teachers undertaking narrative inquiry with children. *Analytic Teaching, 12*(2), 9 - 18.

Ellis, J. L. (1993). "If I were a boy . . .": Constructing knowledge about gender issues in teacher education. *Curriculum Inquiry, 23*(4), 367 - 394.

Ellis, J. L. (1994). Narrative inquiry with children: A generative form of preservice teacher research. *International Journal for Qualitative Studies in Education, 7*(4), 367-380.

Florio-Ruane, S. (1991). Conversation and narrative in collaborative research. In C. Witherell & N. Noddings (eds.), *Stories lives tell* (pp. 234-256). New York: Teachers College Press.

Gergen, K.J. & Gergen, M.M. (1987). The self in temporal perspective. In R. Abeles (ed.), *Life-span perspectives and social psychology* (pp. 121-137). Hillsdale, N.J.: Lawrence Erlbaum Associates.

Harre, R. & Gillet, G. (1994). *The discursive mind*. London: Sage Publications.

MacIntyre, A. (1981). *After virtue: A study in moral theory*. Southbend, IN: University of Notre Dame Press.

Polkinghorne, D.E. (1988). *Narrative knowing and the human science*. Albany: SUNY Press.

Potter, J. & Wetherell, M. (1987). *Discourse and social psychology: Beyond attitudes and behaviour*. London: Sage Publications.

Sarbin, T.R. (Ed.). (1986). *Narrative psychology: The storied nature of human conduct*. New York: Praeger.

van Manen, M. (1984). Practising phenomenological writing. *Phenomenology and Pedagogy*, *4*(2),36-69.

Wetherell, M. & Potter, J. (1988). Discourse analysis and the identification of interpretive repertoires. In C.Antaki (ed.), *Analysing everyday explanations: A casebook of methods*. Beverly Hills, CA: Sage Publications.

Appendix A Interview Schedule
1. If you had to go to school only three days a week, what are some of the things you'd like to do with the extra time?
2. Have you ever done anything that other people were surprised you could do?
3. What's the most difficult thing you've ever had to do or, is there something you've done that was really hard to do but you really wanted to do it?
4. Some people really believe in the power of wishing. Do you think you do? . . . [The ellipsis indicates a follow-up to a response.] Has it ever worked?
5. Do you ever get other people to go along with your ideas or what you want to do? What about in activities with friends or activities or routines at home?
6. Sometimes we like to day-dream about things we'd like to do, or things we'd like to try, or things we'd like to become. Can you remember anything you've ever day-dreamed about?
7. Have you ever done anything really different from what most people your age have done, made something, read up on something, planned something, tried something?
8. Some people believe that willpower can take them a long way. Do you think that you've ever used willpower?
9. I'm going to ask you some different kinds of questions now, questions about how you see things. For example, who do you think makes the biggest difference to what happens in the classroom, the principal, the teacher, or the students?
10. When people disagree over something, why do you think that usually is?
11. What things would you say are most important in life to most people? . . . What do you think will be most important in life to you?
12. In all of the things you're interested in or you've thought about a lot, what has puzzled you the most?
13. What's the best thing about being your age? . . . What's the hardest thing about being your age?
14. What would you like to be really good at doing?

15. If you could pick one thing that you wouldn't have to worry about anymore, what would it be? . . . What would be the next thing?
16. In the world of nature or in the world of things or in the world of people, what is it that surprises you the most, or that you find the most fascinating?
17. Some people really believe in the power of prayer. Do you think that you do?
18. Some people always have lots of ideas at their fingertips. You know, they always have lots of ideas about what to get someone for a present, or they find it really easy to think of things to say in a story they have to write or a letter. Other people have to work really hard to come up with ideas, or they just seem to come more slowly. Which kind of person sounds more like you? . . . Can you think of an example of when you had lots of ideas or when you had trouble thinking of ideas?
19. Can you remember any time when you've run into a difficulty when you were trying to do something or make something or something you needed was missing, something got in the way or slowed things down? . . . What did you do?
20. Can you think of anything that's a constant nuisance or that always annoys you? . . . What are some of the things you've tried to do about it?
21. What do you do when you need a really good idea?
22. If you could spend two weeks with someone who does a special kind of work, what kind of person would that be?
23. In the year ahead, what are some of the things you'd like to accomplish or try for the first time?
24. Is there anyone you see as a kind of hero or heroine, someone you look up to and would like to be like?
25. Do you spend very much time writing or drawing? . . . Have you ever been in a play?
26. Is there something that you've always wanted to do but you haven't had the chance yet? . . . What stopped you, no time, or materials, or resources?

Appendix B: Sample Consent Letter for Parents

                                                        Date
Internal Address

Dear Parent or Guardian:

I am a professor in the Department of Elementary Education at the University of Alberta and am inviting the student
teachers I work with to interview one child, nine years of age
or older, as part of their experience of developing their ideas
about teaching. I am writing to ask whether a student teacher
could interview your child.

The student teacher would interview your child asking
such questions as "What's the best thing about being your
age?" "What do you think will be most important in life to
you?" and "If you could spend two weeks with someone who
does a special kind of work, what kind of person would that
be?" I have found that children who participate enjoy the
opportunity to have an adult listen to them talk about things
they're interested in. The interview would be tape recorded so
that the student teacher could play it back in order to write a
summary of his or her new understandings. The tape would
then be erased and no one but the student teacher would have
had access to it. The student teacher would share their written
work with me and with one other student teacher without using
your child's real name.

The purpose of the interview is to help student teachers
learn more about having conversations with children as a way
to understand children's interests, motivations, and aspirations.
This more holistic way of understanding children can help
them plan classroom activities that are well-suited to the
students.

The interview is 45 minutes in length and would be
scheduled for a time that is agreeable to both the teacher and
your child. If you will allow your child to be interviewed,
please complete the form attached and return it to your
child's teacher by _____. If, on the day of the interview,
your child is shy or unwilling, he or she will not have to participate. Should your child wish to change his or her mind about
doing the interview at any time, he or she is free to do so.

I sincerely appreciate your consideration of this request. If you have any questions about the interview assignment, please contact me at (telephone number).

Thank you.

Sincerely,

Julia Ellis
Associate Professor

JE/pk
Enclosure

* * *

Consent Form

NAME   _____

ADDRESS   _____
       _____

     _____
          Postal Code

I DO NOT agree to have my son/daughter _____
                                                 Name
participate in an interview with a student teacher for the interview assignment with Julia Ellis.

Date   _____   Signature _____

OR

I DO agree to have my son/daughter _____
                                                 Name
participate in a taped-recorded interview with a student teacher as part of the interview assignment with Julia Ellis.

Date   _____   Signature _____

Comments:

Appendix C: Guidelines for Conducting the Interview

Time

Allow approximately one hour for the interview. It may take 10 or 15 minutes to settle in, get set up, and explain the purpose of the interview. The interview itself should not exceed 45 minutes; any more time than this is likely to exhaust the child.

Materials

You will need a tape recorder and a 90-minute tape (so that you will have 45 minutes on one side of the tape uninterrupted); a note pad and pen or pencil; and the interview questions. The interview questions should be transferred to 3" x 5" file cards (one question per card) and the file cards should be held together with two rings. (This way you won't lose your place in the interview schedule and the child won't be tempted to read the questions upside-down.)

Introduction

Explain that the purpose of the interview is to help you "understand how people your age see things, what's important to them, what they're interested in, what their opinions or ideas are." Explain that you would like to record the interview so that you can play it back to yourself later in order to write about the understandings you've gained. Assure the child that no one else will listen to the tape except you. Ask the child if it's okay with him or her if you record the interview. Also advise the child that you'll be jotting down notes during the interview to help you remember what was talked about in case the tape is difficult to hear in places.

During the Interview

Take notes if you can while still concentrating on the conversation. Use probing (but not prying) questions to encourage the child to flesh out more complete stories or talk more about obviously exciting events or ideas important to him or her. (Here is an example of a probing question: "How did you come to be interested in playing the piano?" Here is an example of a prying question: "Do either of your parents play an instrument?")

Appendix D: Three Probing Questions for Reflection

1. How were your conceptions of this particular child or youth, or children and youth in general, altered by this narrative inquiry experience? What did you learn? What surprised you? To what did you become more sensitized? Did any new concerns or questions surface for you? (Answering these kinds of questions may require some overlap or redundancy with the narrative portrait itself. This is as it should be. The reflections section should be an opportunity to pull together and perhaps extend the kinds of insights or thoughts you developed in the narrative portrait.)

2. How was your own self-awareness altered by this narrative inquiry experience? Did you discover or notice anything about your own capabilities, predispositions, or self-identity? Did you become more sensitized to anything important to you or your usual way of thinking about things?

3. How did this experience contribute to your own convictions, concerns, or aspirations for future classroom practice or teaching philosophy?

Appendix E: Parent Interview Schedule

1. As _____ has gotten older, would you say he (or she) has changed a lot or stayed the same?
2. How would you say that _____ is different from brothers or sisters, or from friends?
3. What does _____ do when he can't figure something out right away?
4. Does _____ ever find unusual ways to do things?
5. Would you say that _____ is a child who always has lots to say, lots of ideas, questions, or suggestions?
6. What does _____ usually do when he gets stumped or blocked when he's working on something, trying to make something, get something, go somewhere? What does _____ do when things try his patience, like the usual rules or routines or constant sources of annoyance?
7. Some children believe strongly in the power of wishing, do you think _____ does?
8. Would you say that _____ is very good at getting his way? You know, is he pretty good at tapping any "soft spots"?
9. Is _____ ever the initiator of family activities or new ways of doing things around the home?
10. Is _____ ever the one to initiate activities with friends?
11. Has _____ ever surprised you with his capabilities, or initiative, or staying power?
12. Has _____ ever done anything else that was extremely difficult or complicated or that required endurance.
13. Does _____ have any unusual or interesting aspirations, plans or dreams?
14. Do you think _____ is aware of the idea of willpower or that he ever uses it?
15. Sometimes children surprise us with their depth of understanding or how much they know about things. Does _____ ever make comments or ask questions that surprise you in that way?
16. Would you say that _____ has good analytic ability? Can you think of any examples of where you noticed it?
17. Would you say that _____ is particularly perceptive, or sensitive or thoughtful?
18. What is _____ most curious about or fascinated with?

19. What kinds of things does _____ find easy to do or hard to do?
20. Some children believe in the power of prayer. Do you think that _____ does?
21. What would you say are _____'s strongest interests? How long has he held them, how does he pursue them, and what related projects does he engage in?
22. Whenever _____ is really excited to tell you about something, what is it usually about?
23. What does _____ usually do when someone else is trying to do something or fix something?
24. Are there any older children or adults _____ likes to spend time with? What do they do or talk about together?

Chapter Four

Creative Assignments That Promote Learning and Understanding

Julia Ellis

Introduction

During four years in a teacher education program in Toronto, I asked more than 450 student teachers to design creative assignments for their practicum classes and to research and report on the results of these activities. In studying their reports, I came to see that in spite of the diversity of activities the student teachers assigned their students, all of these assignments served in some way to help the teacher understand their students' realities and then respond to this new awareness.

Teachers can incorporate whatever they learn about their students' fears, loves, interests, talents, beliefs, experiences, aspirations or preoccupations into their practical reasoning about "appropriate action" to take with students and in planning a curriculum. A number of writers (for example, Grundy, 1982; Carr and Kemmis, 1986; Elliot, 1987; and Feldman, 1991) have argued that the kind of knowing, reasoning, and acting teaching represents is or should be characterized primarily by practical judgment rather than by technical knowledge (knowing how) or scientific knowledge (knowing that). Practical reasoning is understood as a disposition to "act well" or to take "good or moral action" on the basis of sound deliberation that considers all of one's knowledge, values, and contextual circumstances. While a teacher's deliberation may be informed by generalizations, propositions, or maxims, these must usually be abandoned or modified in the face of uncertain problems (Feldman, 1991). As Grundy (1982) observed, the idea of "right action" or *praxis* is necessarily "personal, subjective, and never fully formed, always in a state of being formed" (p. 27). Gadamer (1989) used the terms "judgment" and "taste" to refer to the choosing of actions that are "fitting" (p. 38). Curriculum planning models routinely depict a teacher's "knowledge of students" as an influential component. I have often seen what I call "creative assignments" (actually, advanced research activities) produce important and useful insights into students. While research may be an appealing prospect for many teachers, most forms of it are too time- and labor-intensive to be realistic. Researching the creative assignments students complete, however, can help teachers toward increased awarenesses within a manageable research period.

In today's classrooms, teachers must continually find ways to engage and promote the learning of increasingly diverse student populations. In fact, "Inclusive Education" was the recent theme for both the annual graduate summer institute in education at my own university and the Canadian Association for the Study of Women and Education Summer Institute. If we acknowledge that teaching and pedagogy depend as much on cordial and respectful relationships with students and a knowledge of those students as on technical skill, then the value of the kinds of activities described in this chapter will be apparent.

This chapter provides an overview of how student teachers undertake their "creative assignment research." Then it discusses three themes I have associated with understanding student realities in my study of student teachers' reports on these activities. The three themes are

1. recognizing play as a space for children's realities

2. connecting with kids and building community, and

3. being moved to "right action."

Creative Assignment Research
To help them design creative assignments, I invite my student teachers to follow one of the following three formats:

FORMAT 1—FORCED CONNECTION CREATIVE ASSIGNMENTS: This format encourages a teacher to connect a curriculum topic and a topic of current interest to students in order to develop a playful or fanciful activity that also includes a review of the curriculum topic. For example, one student teacher was concluding a unit on the topic of farms in a first grade class as Halloween approached. She invited the class to make three-dimensional models of what witches' farms might look like. In preparation, they made one idea tree showing everything they knew about farms and another showing everything they knew about witches. In a sixth grade class concluding a unit on electricity, a teacher asked her students to use the terminology they learned in electricity to write essays about how friendships work. In a high school typing class, during a unit on preparing forms, the students developed application forms for potential life partners to complete for them.

Figure 1:
Format 1—Forced Connections Creative Assignments

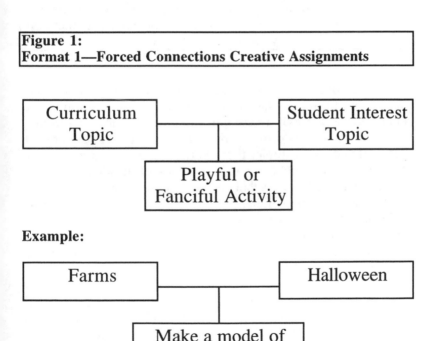

Example:

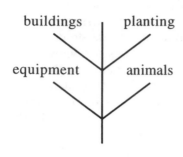

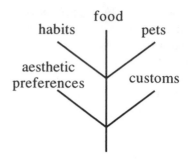

Idea Tree for Farms   **Idea Tree for Witches**

Other Examples:	•Use the terminology from electricity to write essay about how friendships work. •In typing/keyboarding prepare application forms for potential life partners to complete. •In accounting prepare financial statements to show your use of lottery winnings.

FORMAT 2—IDEA TREES AS INTRODUCTIONS TO TOPICS: Following this second format, a class works together to make an idea tree related to the topic of a new unit of study. In such an activity, the students brainstorm all their knowledge, experience or ideas related to the topic, then work as a group to categorize the ideas onto branches or sub-branches of an idea tree. This activity can alert the teacher to the students' topic-related experiences, interests, beliefs, or concerns, which can then serve as focuses for lessons in the unit. In a sixth grade class beginning a unit on fractions, a student teacher encouraged her students to make an idea tree about the activities and objects in their lives that involve fractions. In a fifth grade class beginning a unit on nutrition, the student teacher led the students in making an idea tree about everything that comes to mind when they think about the word "food." In a high school health class starting a unit on sex education, a student teacher had her all-girl class construct one tree for women and one for men. She did this artfully and sensitively in a theater-style class of 60 students. She first had each student privately write

all the words and phrases that came to mind when she said the word "women." Then she repeated the request for the word "men." After the private writing was completed she took oral contributions, which she recorded on the chalk board. As the girls gathered confidence and support from each other, they drew more and more from their private lists to make their oral contributions.

Figure 2:
Format 2—Making and Using Idea Trees to Introduce a Topic or Unit

Making an idea tree is a two-stage process which requires first brainstorming a large number of ideas, and then categorizing these to make the tree.

(1) Brainstorming ideas
The teacher invites students to share all of their ideas related to a given topic or question. Students are given rules for brainstorming: produce lots of ideas, no criticism of anyone else's ideas, and it's okay to piggyback or add on to someone else's ideas.

If students seem to be running out of ideas or seem to be stuck in one train of thought, the teacher should use her awareness of other possible categories of ideas to offer a prompt in the form of a question. For example, if a second grade class was brainstorming ideas about how to keep track of time at home without a clock, and all of their ideas involved using the kitchen, a useful prompt might be: "All of these ideas take place in the kitchen. Does anyone have ideas that would use other parts of a home?"

If some students are shy to volunteer ideas in front of the class, the first stage of the brainstorming could be done in small groups.

Brainstorming sessions invite greater student participation when students can be expected to have related experiential knowledge and the question does not feel test-like. For example, "What are all the different ways people use water?" is preferable to "What are all the things we learned about the water treatment plant?" Similarly, "What are all the ways that

---

cities can be the same or different from each other?" is preferable to "What are all the things you know about the city we are going to study?"

(2) Categorizing the ideas to make the tree
To begin the formation of the idea tree, the teacher asks students to identify ideas that are the same in some way and records each grouping of ideas onto its own branch of the tree. An idea can belong to more than one category and can therefore be used on more than one branch.

As each branch is formed, the teacher asks students to suggest a label or phrase that indicates the subtopic represented by the ideas on the branch. The teacher tries to use the students' own words for naming branches rather than moving too quickly to language that is yet to be introduced. As each branch is named, the teacher can invite brainstorming of additional ideas that can belong on the branch. Once all branches are named, the teacher can invite brainstorming of the names of additional branches that could belong on the tree. Making the idea tree creates awareness of the categories of ideas that exist within the brainstormed list of ideas. Awareness of the categories supports the brainstorming of additional specific ideas within those categories as well as entirely new categories.

(3) Ways to use completed idea trees
The teacher can use a completed idea tree in a number of ways depending on the topic and anticipated instructional activities and assignments. The following are some of the possibilities.

A. The teacher might use awareness of students' related knowledge and experience to plan activities or examples for lessons in the unit. This could happen in a unit on fractions after having students make an idea tree about all of the ways they use or experience fractions in their everyday lives.

B. The teacher could have the students use the tree as a topic outline for individual or group research projects. This would work well in a unit on animals after the students had made an idea tree about all the ways that animals can be the same or different from each other.

C. The tree could serve as a summary and organizer for further information and ideas to be acquired during the course of the unit. For example, a student teacher began a unit on grammar in a French language class by asking the sixth grade students to brainstorm all the French words they knew and to organize them on a tree. The tree enabled them to see the grammatical structures they were already using and provided an organizer they could add to as they acquired more knowledge in the unit.

D. In some instances, the topic of the tree might be much larger than the subtopic that is in fact the focus of the unit. For example, when starting a unit on nutrition, the teacher might have students make an idea tree about about food. While nutrition or healthy eating might be only one branch on the idea tree, the tree would serve to locate the unit within the structure of the larger topic of food. Students also can find it satisfying to present their related knowledge, beliefs and interests at the beginning of their work with a topic. Further, the tree can be saved and used as a reference for thematically related projects in other subject areas such as art, mathematics or social studies.

FORMAT 3—"WHAT IF . . ." ASSIGNMENTS: This third format invites students to respond to a personal or fanciful "What if . . ." situation. In such assignments, students might be asked to draw pictures or diagrams of an ideal bedroom, playground, classroom, and so forth. Stories are often used to initiate other fanciful activities—for example, "What if you were the character in the story who had just found the magic wand that grants a wish? What would you wish for? Draw a picture."

Figure 3:
Format 3—"What if. . ." Assignments

These activities provide an opportunity to learn either students' generally held preoccupations or their beliefs and concerns that pertain to a particular topic.

Using Stories as Starters for Wishful Thinking
Activities that invite the expression of wishes provide an outlet for the expression of general preoccupations. For example, after reading a book called *Spray for a Friend*, a student teacher asked children to imagine that they found cans of magic spray. She asked them to draw pictures of their cans of magic spray and to tell her what kind of magic the cans had. Many picture books or stories can be used in this "story starter" way for self-expressive activities.

Using Wishful Visualization of Familiar Sites
Making drawings or diagrams of idealized versions of familiar settings can also provide an opportunity for students to express interests and aspirations. Examples of such activities can be drawing pictures of ideal classrooms, bedrooms, playgrounds, or cities.

Imagining Oneself Solving
Problems Related to a Curriculum Topic
Many "What if . . . " activities take the form of asking students to imagine that they have a particular role or job and to tell or show what they would do in that role. These activities can help the teacher to learn students' beliefs, knowledge and values that are related to an up-coming topic in the curriculum. Examples are: "Begin a story with the sentence 'If I were president . . . ,'" "Work in a group to make a three-dimensional construction of an imaginary machine that would help with pollution problems," "Design the contents of a James Bond-type briefcase that would help the city's mayor with his or her job," and "Write a proposal for a solution to the rain forest problem." The students' discussions, products, and oral reports can reveal concerns, beliefs, misconceptions or gaps in knowledge related to the curriculum topic.

Next, to "research" the creative assignment activity, student teachers were asked

1. to record during the activity their observations of their students' responses to the activity, to each other, and to the student teacher;

2. to write descriptions of each of the students' products or the oral reports on their products;

3. to identify themes or patterns across students' products and within sub-groups of students (girls, boys, cultural groups, etc.);

4. to identify the value of the activity for the students and for the teacher; and

5. to note their own ideas, questions, concerns, and speculations in the form of reflections on the study.

Recognizing Play as a Space for Children's Realities
Many of the creative assignments given to K-3 children resemble opportunities for focused play in that they involve invention, make-believe, or fantasy. Children generally respond to them with enthusiasm and eagerness. Here are five examples:

HALLOWEEN BEAR BOOGIE PARTY (kindergarten): Students made models, murals, games, and other artifacts to show how bears would celebrate Halloween.

HALLOWEEN SAFETY (grade 1): Students picked a Halloween safety rule and made a Halloween character who would be good at teaching that rule.

THE WITCH FARM (grade 1): After a unit on farms, the class made a witches' farm.

MONSTERS (grade 2): After a unit on the environment, children used recycled "junk" to make monsters.

MONSTER HOMES (grade 3): To conclude a unit on homes and habitats, the students built homes for monsters.

What consistently impressed the student teachers was the way these activities effortlessly evoked from the children so many of the behaviors, skills, and attitudes they hoped for in their work with all children. Their reports invariably expressed their surprise and pleasure in the students' enthusiasm, confidence, productivity, focus, perseverance, social skills, and language use. The children worked hard, happily and maturely at their "play."

We know only a little about what children know, think, and can imagine, and the constant temptation is to look only for our own words or the text's words to come back to us from the children. These creative activities provide a space where children can engage both what they know and what they can think, dream, or imagine. In too much of their lives, children experience themselves only as receptacles for adult agendas. But in these activities, children can explore their own ideas using modes of expression and production that appeal to and satisfy them.

The student teachers typically ask their classes to generate ideas as a whole group before starting on these projects. What they witness in their children's responses and ideas is usually remarkable. A student teacher wrote these comments about her third grade class brainstorming about monster homes:

> They were excited about the topic. I was constantly jolted by the extraordinarily broad spectrum from which the children drew their brainstorming data unfettered by conventional systems and adult-commonsense rules. I found this inspiring and energizing.

In the second grade class where children made monsters from "junk," the student teacher noted that the children had many more ideas about monsters than they did about the environment and that they "really seemed to like giving answers, having them accepted and then written down." In the kindergarten class with the Halloween Bear Boogie Party, the student teacher had this to say about the class response during brainstorming:

[T]he children generated so many outstanding and creative ideas that it was difficult to contain them. . . . They were literally dancing in the hall showing me the bears' dance.

Perhaps these imagination activities signal to students that, at least for a time, we are trying to free them rather than contain them, and this may be why the everyday "behavior problems" disappear when students work on these projects. When students sense that no one is trying to control them, they are quite capable of controlling themselves.

In report after report, my student teachers remark on their students' excitement and engagement throughout the project work. All of the children are happy, focused, and competent in their work. None of them complain, avoid, resist, copy, fight with others, or do a "rush job." They are serious about their own and others' work. They readily share prized and scarce materials. They find diplomatic ways to ask each other for what they need. They strike compromises independently and spontaneously when difficulties occur. They complete much of their work collaboratively or cooperatively. They endeavor to make their products "just right." The student teachers provide many examples of how students demonstrate their pride in their work. These play-like work activities seem very much like Freinet's (1993) conception of "work-play." He suggested that this ideal form of activity satisfies

> our most powerful natural needs: intelligence; deep unity with nature; adaptation to our physical and mental capacities; the feeling of power, of creation and of control; immediately visible practical outcomes; obvious familial and social utility; and a wide range of emotions, including pain, fatigue and suffering. (p. 206)

Within "work-play" activities, Freinet (1993) observed, children experience "a clearly visible goal; easily measureable progress; comparative autonomy for the participants, within the limits of adult requirements; individual satisfaction; and approval from those around us" (p. 185). Without "work-play" activities, children turn to "play-work" activities— activities in which children imitate and practice the work of adults. If opportunities for "play-work" are also blocked, Freinet suggested that children attempt to release their frustration through "various forms of compensatory play." Since my student teachers all observe that their children refrain from "playing around" when they work on their creative assignments, the assignments appear to be examples of the meaningful, independent, creative, and rewarding "work-play" forms of activity Freinet conceptualized.

The childrens' biggest concern is always finishing their products, and days after starting, they will ask if they can continue with these projects. Even after a weekend, kindergarten children would express concern about time being scheduled for further project work. Students are concerned about finishing them "right." The products are real to them —manifestations of their own imaginations, ideas and intentionalities.

The students' next largest concern is to be able to share their products with the class. Frequently they "demand" to share, even those who are normally reticent about presenting to the class. As one student teacher commented, their products were "alive with meaning" for them. Many student teachers express their pleasure about the amount of oral language these activities stimulated and the quality of the writing work often used to extend them.

Sometimes students ask if they can complete more activities in these same ways. Sometimes student teachers conclude that the children need more of these kinds of opportunities in view of the strength of their responses and the richness of language and group learning the activities support. One student teacher related these activities to a child's natural need to learn through play and to work in challenging ways with the imagination. She noted her students' various avoidance strategies in reading, writing, and math and concluded that

> Certainly, in light of this assignment it makes sense to provide children with more creative and imaginative projects of this nature which challenge the students in meaningful ways. But my observations also led me to believe that the nature or structure of these students' other academic work (their reading, writing and math) should be reconsidered and perhaps restructured using what has been learned from this assignment to provide learning experiences for them that are more closely related to their needs and reality.

These creative assignments, meanwhile, gave the student teachers insights into the children's realities and gave the children productive access to their own realities. As the student teachers listened to their students' oral reports and listened in on group work conversations, they heard what the children knew, believed, and cared about in regard to the topics connected to the project. The children thrived in this special space where they could be productive and competent using everything they knew or could imagine. One student teacher in a first grade class met many of the parents after she had been at work only two weeks. The parents of one girl told her that they routinely ask their daughter what she did in school each day and that she routinely answers: "Nothing." Since the student teacher had arrived she was loving school and more frequently replied: "We did brainstorming today and I had lots of ideas."

Connecting With Kids and Building Community
Student teachers working with younger students commonly report, but express no surprise that children had spontaneously approached them to show or tell what they had made in creative assignment activities. Similarly, student teachers working with older students find creative assignment activities to be significant for them. For example, a student teacher in an eighth grade classroom had students draw and label diagrams or pictures of their ideal bedroom. She reported that this one fifteen-minute activity enabled the students to "warm-up" to her and to each other. Students often interpret these creative or expressive activities as invitations to let others see and know them in ways that transcend the usual classroom boundaries. My student teachers' reports suggest that students welcome and respond to these invitations. Here is an excerpt from the report of a student teacher who invited tenth grade students to design studio apartments that would reflect who they were:

> I did not foresee this assignment as directly or indirectly contributing to a sense of community in the classroom, but much to my surprise it did. Students who under normal circumstances would not usually speak to each other were comparing, sharing, and exchanging ideas openly and freely. As the students worked on the

assignment in class, they spoke loudly and one could easily detect the excitement and passion in their voices. Fascination and animation permeated the classroom and an incredible warmth and enthusiasm transmitted from each student.

. . . Furthermore, this type of activity does in fact provide the students with a means of expressing themselves not only as students but also as people, and because it is such a personalized task, it also provides a safe outlet for self-disclosure. We as teachers can gather so much insight into our students via their work (as I have in conducting this particular activity) precisely because the end-products are a reflection and thus a transmission of self that we must come to know and understand in order to ensure communication and sincerity between ourselves and the student. In this particular case, I had students who at first felt threatened and intimidated by me because I was someone new invading their "real" teacher's territory, approach me and share their innovative ideas, justifying why they would have certain things in their living area and how these things were indicative of the sort of people they were. It was absolutely wonderful to see how quickly they were able to generate ideas, how proud they were of them, but especially how willing they were to make me part of their optimism and geniality. This is one experience I will never forget.

Student teachers completing their practicum in secondary classrooms often start to see "30 individuals" instead of "a class." Their students' distinctive responses to creative assignments give student teachers a chance to appreciate and remember more of each student's individuality. Even an assignment like "changing the location or setting of a story, making a picture of the new setting and characters, and writing how the story would be different" gave a student teacher more appreciation of each student's distinctiveness.

The creative assignments also enable the students to appreciate each other more fully. A student teacher in a ninth grade class asked her students to work in groups to create dramatic skits as a follow-up to a reading assignment. Both she and the students were surprised at the leadership ability some students not known for their proficiency in regular class work displayed. The other students' new appreciation of these classmates was palpable, and the newly appreciated students received a boost in their self-esteem. A new appreciation of each other's talents also occurred in the kindergarten Halloween Bear Boogie Party as children in groups decided who would do the printing, draw the bears, or build the furniture, according to each child's skills and interests. To experience community and belonging, each student needs to feel "known" or "seen" and "accepted." The open-ended, creative assignments typically provide a larger space for students to discover and value each other's gifts.

Student teacher reports on creative assignments also acknowledge the value of having students create visual products. Some examples of topics that require these visual products include an ideal town, one's actual or ideal world, and a poster displaying the components of an imagined trip in a particular country or city. One student teacher wrote that six weeks after the practicum, the posters still brought to mind the faces of the students who had created them. Several student teachers mentioned that, during the practicum itself, each time they saw a student's face they also saw the visual product that student had created.

While student teachers acknowledge that the visual products reveal common concerns or interests of the students as a group, they emphasize that each product also reveals something of the unique personality, gifts, or preoccupations of each student. Since a strong visual image may be easier to recall than pages of handwritten text in a class of 30 students, the self-expressive visual products may be particularly useful at the beginning of one's time with that class. Without such memorable and informative signatures, students can offer only their classroom behavior, academic performances, and physical appearances to distinguish themselves from one another. But the visual products reveal a variety of talents, skills, interests, values, knowledge, and preoccupations that can compel the teacher's respect, appreciation, and understanding for students who might have no other means of asserting themselves in the usual classroom activities.

In a variety of ways, these creative assignments give student teachers a chance to befriend and get to know their students as complex, multi-faceted people. In the course of these activities, students also share themselves with each other and respond to the mutuality of that sharing. Creative assignments that require group work make strong contributions to

community and friendships. Many educators expect cooperative group work with structured comprehension and application tasks to build community. Sometimes, however, student relationships deteriorate instead when some students avoid doing
their share on graded projects. In creative assignments, however, the opportunities for fun and conceptual playfulness inherent in their activities encourage the bonding and camara-
derie we would wish for our students. A student teacher in a
seventh grade class described how several members of the
class were social isolates who seemed alienated from their classmates. After giving them group work in a creative assignment
in social studies, she noted that the previous "loners" started
to associate at recess and assemblies with the students in their
groups. In a tenth grade French class, a student teacher asked
the students to work in groups to invent activities for a celebration of Groundhog Day. One group invented a dance and
song they taught the class. Another group invented a game for
the class to play. The class spirit this activity established made
a large contribution to the sense of community in the class.
When students feel "at home" in the classroom, when they
feel connected to the other students and the teacher, they
become more willing to experience the classroom as part of
their reality.

Being Moved to "Right Action"
Many of the student teachers' creative activities brought to the
surface real concerns, preoccupations, and challenges that students were experiencing outside or at home. While the three-
week practicum block typically restricted the student teachers'
follow-up opportunities, I was impressed and even moved by
the desire they expressed to act upon their knowledge and the
many ideas they had for helpful action.

Sometimes the difficulties student teachers discovered
were those of individual students, small groups of students, or
much of the class. In the twelfth grade social studies class
where the teacher asked her students to make posters repre-
senting their ideal and actual worlds, one student used part of
his poster to reveal his dilemma: his need to quit school to
augment the family finances. A student teacher asked her
third grade students to write letters telling someone how to

take care of the magic seed they were offering as a gift. Almost all of the students wrote their letters to other children in the class. But one girl wrote her letter to herself, confiding to the teacher that she knew no one to write to. Some of the boys used only an ordering tone and threats in their letters. The student teacher reviewed and reflected on her other daily observations of the children when interpreting the significance of their approaches to the task.

As a follow-up to the book *The Witch of Lok Island* by Elsie Masson, a student teacher in a third grade class asked her students to imagine that they each owned a magic staff that could help anyone with problems or difficulties. She asked them to illustrate whom they would help or what situations they would try to correct. While most of the class focused on such social issues as hunger, pollution, or crime, a few used this activity to express their concern about sick or deceased relatives, reuniting families, or improving the climate in blended families. The student teacher suddenly had abundant ideas about how to follow up and provide support for those students with difficulties and concerns. She also emphasized her appreciation of the importance of giving children the freedom to put their fears and troubles into words.

A student teacher in another third grade read *Johnny Maple Leaf* to the class. At the point in the story where the leaf is about to fall to the ground she stopped the story and asked the class where they would like to go, or what they would do, if they were a leaf and could float absolutely anywhere and do anything. She was surprised to find that of the 22 compositions she received, 14 were about visiting the parents' country of origin, and of these, eight involved getting to meet parents' friends and relatives. Some of the stories expressed the belief that these places are nice because people help each other there.

As a final example of discovering students' concerns and difficulties, I draw from the report of a student teacher I will call Carol. Carol offered a creative assignment to a ninth grade advanced English class, a group she described as "difficult." Since the students were about to read a futuristic science fiction novel that presents an unusual system of education, she took a period to have the students develop their own versions of "ideal education systems."

Carol was initially struck by how "involved and attentive" the students became during the warm-up (brainstorming and the formation of an idea tree), the writing, and the brief discussion at the end. When she analyzed their written submissions, Carol found that they divided naturally into two groups. One group (about half the class) "presented a string of negatives destroying the system as we know it (that is to say, no teachers, no principals, no homework, no classes except one day a month, no school after sixth grade, etc.) but putting nothing in its place." The other half "maintained the system as we have it but suggested ways of improving it." Carol feared that the students in the first group might be at risk of dropping out if nothing changed in the next couple years. She was also alarmed that good behavior and good marks were no guarantee against dropping out since some of the best students were in the group expressing the greatest unhappiness. This excerpt from Carol's report reveals what she would want to do:

> What I would definitely like to introduce into this classroom, given what I saw during the assignment, are classroom meetings to be held every two weeks or so. I would leave thirty to forty-five minutes at the end of a period open so that students could bring up anything of concern or interest to them, and it would not have to be limited to what is happening in the actual course.

Like Carol, other student teachers completing this assignment identified how they acted or would want to act upon what they had learned about their students. Sometimes they insisted that the students had to be listened to more. More frequently they planned further class activities incorporating the identified interests, concerns or needs of students while also serving the required purposes of the course. Sometimes they wanted to go back to the students and engage them in dialogues about the meaning or significance of patterns or themes in their creative products. These represented practical judgments from student teachers in the first three months of their teacher education program.

Discussion

A recurring theme throughout my student teachers' reports is their awareness of how uncommon or unusual students find these creative activities. Sometimes supervising teachers warned the student teachers that the students would be incapable of handling the tasks or controlling their behavior during the tasks. Yet all K-12 students proved capable. Many stories emerged about classroom teachers expressing pride and pleasure in the students' accomplishments and in the accompanying oral and written language. Sometimes the classroom teacher called in the principal or other teachers to see the students' products or witness their intensity and concentration.

Seeking to explain how activities like those the student teachers assigned could alienate the more traditional education professionals, I thought about the insights of authors who have worked to make sense of trends in our schools. In his review of the history of teaching methods, Connell (1987) observed the persistent tendency for *educational methods or approaches* to be transformed into *instructional patterns*. Since teaching professionals like routines and efficiency, instructional patterns tend to dominate. In fact, Connell concluded that the history of teaching methods can be seen as a history of instructional patterns from which the teaching profession must be periodically rescued. He also noted the influences of habituation and zeitgeists. Teachers tend to teach the same ways they saw themselves to have been successfully taught. Authentic changes in teaching have all been associated with wider social and cultural changes or current zeitgeists.

In offering an analysis of observations in a kindergarten, Apple and King (1977) noted how the procedures, routines, and teacher talk in the class all served to emphasize the goals of children becoming obedient, following instructions, restraining themselves, tolerating discomfort, and completing tasks on schedule. From these emphases, children quickly learned the difference between work and play. They were learning to adjust to what the demands of the work place might be. While various zeitgeists have come and gone over the recent decades, many of today's teachers still carry with them the uninterrogated hidden curriculum of their own years as students in schools, and their implicit assumptions about the bipolarity of work and play could discourage more inventive teachers from employing creative assignments.

Just as the work-play dichotomy discourages the use of creative assignments, so too, what Lilia Bartolome (1994) calls the "methods fetish" can distract teachers from their own creative role in pedagogy. Bartolome pointed out that even student teachers expect to learn "one size fits all recipes" for effectively teaching subordinated learners. She emphasized, however, that there are no roads but the one we create as we walk it together and that even unsophisticated methods can work when students feel genuinely respected, known, and appreciated by the teacher. Adopting the kinds of creative assignments discussed in this chapter, teachers can increase their opportunities to recognize and appreciate what students care about, know, have experienced, and can do. Knowing their students' realities can inspire the teacher's imagination and encourage a teacher's inclination to take "right action."

References

Apple, M.W. & King, N.R. (1977). What do schools teach? *Curriculum Inquiry, 6*(4), 341-358.

Bartolome, L.I. (1994). Beyond the methods fetish: Toward a humanizing pedagogy. *Harvard Educational Review, 64*(2), 173-194.

Carr, W. & Kemmis, S. (1986). Becoming critical: Education, knowledge, and action research. Philadelphia, PA: Falmer Press, Taylor & Francis Inc.

Connell, W.F. (1987). History of teaching methods. In M.J. Dunkin (ed.), *The international encyclopedia of teaching and teacher education,* (pp. 201-214). New York: Pergamon Press.

Elliot, J. (1987). Teachers as researchers. In M.J. Dunkin (ed.), *International encyclopedia of teaching and teacher education*, (pp. 162-164). New York: Pergamon Press.

Feldman, A. (1991). Teacher knowledge and practical reasoning. Paper presented at the first Invitational Symposium on Teacher Education, Spencer Hall, University of Western Ontario.

Freinet, C. (1993). *Education through work: A model for child-centered learning. (J. Sivell, trans.).* New York: Edwin Mellen Press. (Original work published 1960)

Gadamer, H-G. (1989). *Truth and method, second revised edition. (J. Weinsheimer & D. G. Marshall, trans.).* New York: The Publishing Corporation.

Grundy, S. (1982). Three modes of action research. *Curriculum Perspectives, 2*(3), 23-34.

PART TWO

TEACHERS' INTERPRETIVE INQUIRIES

Chapter Five

About Alex

Miriam Shell

> The future is not some place we are going to, but one we are
> creating. The paths are not to be found, but made, and the activity
> of making them changes both the maker and the destination.
> (John Schaar, as cited in T.J. Sergiovanni, 1994, p.187)

Introduction

Self appraisal is both a path towards personal understanding
and growth and an imperative in a profession like teaching
that expects its practitioners to maintain a complimentary
public image, to exhibit excellent communication, and to produce education results of all kinds. Teachers who fail to
exercise some form of self appraisal can hardly be effective in
their jobs. Educators and academics interested in exploring
this aspect of professional development often call it *reflective
practice* or *teaching as research* (Paley, 1986; Elliott, 1987;
Avery, 1990; Lieberman, 1990; McConaghy, 1990; White,
1990; Henderson, 1992; Smyth, 1992; Shute and Gibb, 1993).

This chapter begins with my own anxiety as I tried to cope
with and learn from a particularly puzzling and difficult student. By paying even closer attention than usual to who I am
and what I do as a teacher, I hoped to improve my teaching.
By reflecting specifically on how I worked with Alex (a
pseudonym) and his classmates one particular year, I hoped to
learn and grow as a practitioner. Accordingly, I focused on
both the process and perceived growth that occurred when I
taught Alex in the first grade and applied my newly acquired
ideas about reflective practice.

At university part time during the first year of my M. Ed.
program, I read about reflective practice, postmodern think-

ing, and feminist pedagogy while continuing to work as a class-room teacher. As I studied and struggled to help my students, I looked for a context or framework for locating my teaching decisions and for validating or interrogating my choices of teaching strategies.

At the time, I had a teaching assignment in an urban elementary school that offered a bilingual program in a heritage language. Most children attending the school did so for cultural reasons as the language taught was key to pre-serving and participating in the culture of their community. The children spent half the school day studying with me in the target language and the other half studying in English. Most of the curriculum was taught in English, while music, social studies, and health were taught in the heritage language. The class of children I describe here remained with me for half of every teaching day. In the other half, I taught another group of first graders who had already studied in English that day.

About Alex

Alex was stocky and large for a boy six. He came bounding into my classroom the first morning, aggressively eager to stake out his territory and dominance. During the first hour he shoved several students out of the way when they stood in his path, shouted expletives when frustrated, and loudly de-manded that his classmates and I meet his demands of the moment.

During the first few weeks of school, Alex remained apart from the group during activities, and failed to complete any of the product-oriented assignments to his or my satisfaction. Instead, he engaged in distracting and destructive behavior. His loud, boisterous movements in my classroom undermined my efforts to create a calm, caring, supportive atmosphere in which students could risk learning.

Alex's apparent obliviousness of lessons in progress and his anti-social behavior soon became evident outside my class-room as well. He became the object of other students' and teachers' complaints, thereby gaining the status of a "high profile" student. On the playground, and in other classes, he often broke such basic rules as "Walk don't run," "Play safe," "Don't hurt others," and "Don't throw stones." In the staff room, the halls, and outside at recess, he became a major topic of discussion.

Alex's misbehavior often involved objects rather than people. On one occasion, he smashed a juice bottle he found on the playground, then ran around waving the piece with jagged edges. On another occasion in class, he carefully cut small slits in his pants with his scissors. Alex would write on desks, drill holes in erasers, scribble on other students' work, tear pages, and throw pencils and chalk. He had difficulty moving among the other children, and they quickly became annoyed and unforgiving of him, if they were not actually fearful.

Observing that I spent too much of my valuable time monitoring Alex's movements, intervening in his difficulties with other children and adults, and supervising his use of materials, I realized that his behavior was consuming my teaching day and controlling my classroom. Feeling my attention, and that of the other students repeatedly distracted from the business of reading and writing and enjoying learning together, I was nevertheless bound by my professional obligation to make school a positive place for Alex. Furthermore, while the routine referrals to appropriate specialists and conferences with colleagues and parents went ahead, I knew I had to regain both control over my class learning environment, and my own sense of balance.

In the foreword to Connie White's (1990) book, *Jevon Doesn't Sit at the Back Anymore*, Jerome Harste wrote that "the teacher-as-researcher movement is an attempt to hear teachers and to support them in the development of their own voices. Teaching-as-inquiry is education at its best" (p. ii). If, as Harste noted, "education begins when learners ask their own questions and then proceed with their own inquiry," and I continue to be a learner even as I teach, then watching and asking what was going on in my own experience was part of my job as a teacher. Moreover, it might generate a discourse with the children and the staff about what was happening with Alex so that we could all learn new ways to come together.

Alex challenged me both to maintain my goals for my other students and to find a door to open that would welcome this child to an appealing world at school. Encouraged to con-

duct the research myself, I began to carefully examine what
was happening. On the one hand, I began to watch Alex with
intentionality, looking for triggers, patterns, and secrets to his
actions. Were they random, impulsive, or premeditated? What
could I learn just by watching him and listening to what he
had to say? On the other hand, I became acutely aware of my
own behavior and experience with Alex in my room. How was
I reacting to the tension he produced, and how was it influencing my attention to the other students? What might I do
consciously and logically to improve the situation? How could
I rally the school's resources to help us include this boy?

An only child, Alex had come to Canada from Eastern
Europe with his parents when he was three, at a time when he
was just learning to express himself. The first year in Canada,
Alex attended an English daycare center and a half-day English summer camp. When he was five, he attended a French
immersion kindergarten and the English daycare center. Upon
entering the Heritage Language Program I taught in the first
grade, Alex had no comfortable language base in his first
language, which he still heard spoken at home, or in English,
or in French. Also, he had never before had any exposure to
the heritage language taught in our school; this was the fourth
language he was being exposed to in his young life.

Alex's report cards from the daycare center and kindergarten both mentioned his "difficult to control" behavior and
his" immature skills." They also recorded qualities I too had
begun to notice. Alex appeared to be bright and curious,
showing that he wanted to learn. He appeared to know his
manners, though he rarely used them, and would take pleasure
in being helpful or in the limelight. I clung to these points
knowing I might capitalize on these positive characteristics to
everyone's advantage.

As I watched and listened to Alex and all those who came
into contact with him, I noticed he was sensitive to touch.
Being a large boy, he demanded a lot of space as he moved
about and was quick to react if jostled or crowded (a perpetual
condition in our overcrowded school). Alex was also sensitive
and hostile to what he perceived as verbal ridicule, intended or
not.

During lessons, Alex neither watched nor appeared to listen. He exhibited such classic avoidance behaviors as taking trips to the washroom, sharpening pencils, tidying his desk, taking longer than usual to get ready, or just having something else to do. On written work, his pencil control was inexperienced, and he put little effort into completing sentences or thoughts. He did watch (from a distance) any learning game we played, and whenever we sang, his eyes brightened, although he did not try to participate. Sadly, most of the time during lessons, Alex managed to disrupt the group in one way or another.

Something About Me
The more I reflected, the more I saw how emotionally distraught I had become with Alex on my mind all the time, in and out of work. I worried about how little mental energy I spent on my other students. I saw them too, wearying of Alex's constant distractions and demands for my attention. I was losing sight of my own program goals and feeling confused about what was happening to me and my class atmosphere. I also realized that I was becoming moody, impatient, and distracted in my dealings with students and colleagues.

Amid my anxiety, I remembered reading I had done about the value of self reflection in improving teaching practice. Edelsky, Draper and Smith (1983) had examined the various roles a teacher assumed in her classroom and the corresponding student behaviors each role prompted or supported. I wanted to examine my own behavior and I decided to review some of my underlying attitudes and beliefs about effective learning and teaching.

Knowing that my beliefs probably determined the roles I assumed in the classroom (for example, policing, preaching, guiding, or stimulating), I hoped that reclaiming my attitudes and beliefs would realign my behavior with my goals. My university studies at the time encouraged me to reflect on my teaching and review a variety of conceptual frameworks or paradigms for teaching. These activities helped me as I struggled to meet Alex's challenge.

Engaged as I was in current research, journal writing, and regular discussions with colleagues, I gradually clarified the beliefs and attitudes I held as a teacher. In fact, it was the supportive academic environment of the university and the opportunity for discourse with colleagues that provided the main impetus for this soul searching.

Attitudes and Beliefs
Succinctly stated, my reflecting led to several conclusions about my attitudes and my beliefs about people and learning. Those attitudes that contribute to, and may be necessary for effective teaching encourage me to be

- trusting and eager to allow participation in class,
- optimistic and happy,
- reassuring and encouraging,
- patient and attentive,
- confident and determined to stick to my principles, and
- questioning and inquisitive.

The beliefs that form the foundation of my teaching practice are that

- all people are or want to be good,
- people are interesting, and
- people are social beings.

About Learning, I believe that

- all people can learn, barring any severe limitations,
- learning must be relevant and connected to life experiences,
- learning occurs non-linearly in fits and starts, and
- people have to feel good about themselves for optimum learning to occur.

Strategies
After I enunciated and listed these underlying concepts, I found it easy to translate my attitudes and beliefs into these three action statements that describe what I wanted to accomplish in the classroom:

1. Empowering students means listening to and trusting their perceptions and solutions to problems.

2. Because people are interesting, their differences are to be valued as opportunities for acceptance and causes for celebration in the social climate of the class.

3. Optimism and happiness help to develop learners who actively embrace life and all its moments, pleasant ones to enjoy, and difficult ones as challenges to meet.

Once I clarified my beliefs about effective teaching and formulated these three general action statements, I wondered how I could realign what was happening between Alex and me, as well as with my other students. Reading and thinking about a variety of paradigms or perspectives prominent in education, I felt assured that current theories supported both my method of approaching my "problem," and my choices of action. Whereas I would have once called my choices hunches, I could now relate my ideas to those of others in my field.

Articles focused on "the teacher as researcher" described others using reflection as a process that validates the sharing of personal voices as a productive professional activity. In her 1990 chapter, "Learning to Research/Researching to Learn," Carol Avery supports my own thoughts and reflections on my teaching: "I write about what I see in order to clarify my observations" (p. 33)—and as I talked about my reflections with colleagues—"The process of that writing enabled us to make connections and discover meanings from our classroom observations and interactions" (p. 37).

My first and perhaps most catalytic change was in my attitude toward Alex himself and toward all my experiences with colleagues and students regarding him. To be true to my beliefs that all people want to be good and that all can learn, I had to relate to Alex as though these ideas were true for him too. By relating to the child patiently and happily, and by encouraging and reassuring him, I saw how I could be true to my own attitudes towards children at the same time as showing him his place in the school environment. In the article, " On Listening To What Children Say," Vivian Paley (1986) wrote,

> As we seek to learn more about a child, we demonstrate the acts of
> observing, listening, questioning, and wondering. When we are
> curious about a child's words and our responses to those words, the
> child feels respected. The child is respected. "What are these ideas I
> have that are so interesting to the teacher? I must be somebody
> with good ideas." Children who know others are listening may
> begin to listen to themselves, and if the teacher acts as the tape
> recorder, they may one day become their own critics (p. 127).

If I was ever to align Alex's behavior with the goals of the
classroom, I knew the motivation would have to come from
Alex himself, ideally as he became his own empowered critic
and decision maker. Rather than relate to Alex sharply and im-
patiently, anticipating trouble at every turn, I consciously for-
gave him his sins (which was hard), and began acting cheerful,
interested, and positive towards him.

As my relationship with him took on a friendly rather than
adversarial tone, my interventions when he misbehaved became more helpful, controlled, and non-verbal. Our sudden,
loud, angry outbursts diminished as a more collaborative discipline plan emerged. The consequences that used to be perceived as punishments began to be re-established by mutual
agreement between Alex and me, though they sometimes
involved the principal and his parents.

As my own attitude changed, I found it easier to encourage and reassure colleagues who continued to have difficulties
with Alex. I explained what we were doing that worked, rather
than just griping with them as I had done before.

In the article just cited, Vivian Paley went on to insist that,
for her, "the first order of reality in the classroom is the student's point of view. . . [and that that] is where the lessons are
to be found" (p. 127). If one can learn from self inquiry and
reflection, one can surely learn from the students themselves
and their own perceptions of their realities.

On Alex's Side

In accordance with my beliefs that people are social beings
and that learning must be relevant or connected somehow to
life experiences, I wanted to engage the whole class in the
group dynamics necessary to help Alex join us and of course,
I wanted to help us all continue our job of learning without so

many disruptive outbursts. Now that I had aligned myself on Alex's side, I had to include the rest of the class in our collaboration. That was the second most important change I implemented in trying to help Alex. Carol Avery (1990) wrote that

> As a teacher-researcher, I became a learner in the classroom concerned with what my students were learning and how they were learning. I experienced the classroom as a collaborative venture and examined not only how I functioned but also how we worked together and why strategies did or did not work (p. 44).

Avery's observation would prove true for me too as I allowed my students to generate solutions and suggest ways to help Alex become a positive group member.

When I told the children my belief that everyone wanted to learn and to belong and my hope that the group would share responsibility for the happiness and learning of all, and then opened a discussion about these ideas, my first grade students rose to the challenge. Over the next few weeks, with my encouragement, they proposed and implemented these three strategies for helping Alex:

1. Alex was welcome in group activities, but he had to earn his way in with good behavior.

2. Alex would have a buddy for friendship and collaborative learning.

3. Alex would get special acknowledgment for proper behavior "because it took him more effort."

As my own attitude and tone in class changed to include Alex as one of us rather than as our nemesis, so did those of my students. Not just allowing but also trusting my students to acquire the problem collectively, I created an atmosphere of acceptance and, for Alex, a sense of inclusion rather than exclusion. He became highly motivated to earn the group's favor through compliance with acceptable behavior patterns and learning efforts, rather than engaging in disruptive attention seeking. Alex's desk was placed somewhat apart from the group, and he had to earn his way to periods with the group by remaining on task. This approach, using isolation from the group in an atmosphere of collective caring and support, proved a strong motivator, as I had suspected it would from reading Alex's earlier report cards.

Around the same time, as I continued my part-time university studies, I read several articles about feminist pedagogy. Again, I heard my own beliefs and consequent actions described by others. I realized that I could gain new outlooks from these various theoretical paradigms, and I learned that in my practice, I had become part of them. In an article entitled, "An Ethic Of Caring," Nel Noddings (1988) wrote that

> The teacher models not only admirable patterns of intellectual activity but also desirable ways of interacting with people. Such teachers treat students with respect and consideration and encourage them to treat each other in a similar fashion. They use teaching moments as caring occasions. . . . In a classroom dedicated to caring, students are encouraged to support each other; opportunities for peer interaction are provided, and the quality of that interaction is as important (to both teacher and students) as the academic outcomes (p. 223).

With the children befriending Alex as often as possible, they began to buddy up with others too. I began to circulate among other students, no longer preoccupied by just one. I could maintain my position of "leader" in the room, paying positive attention to Alex when I chose rather than when he demanded and began to notice the many possibilities for positive interaction in the classroom open up for Alex. Remembering how he responded to games, I used games to start his learning activities. At first, Alex wouldn't participate and only watched others. But after a while, he began to join in. If his behavior was inappropriate, he would be asked to go to his isolated desk, and try again later. At last he had some motivation to accept and join the learning going on in the class.

As the buddies helped, and cooperative learning increased all around, my students celebrated his achievements (and their own), and they were sad when he failed. Alex knew how the rest of the children viewed him. Previously, they avoided him, now they talked with him. Shrewsbury (1987) stated that

> [I]n a feminist classroom, students integrate the skills of critical thinking with respect for and ability to work with others. Feminist pedagogy strives to help student and teacher learn to think in new ways, especially ways that enhance the integrity and wholeness of the person and the person's connections with others (p. 7).

By engaging my students in the process of examining how we all felt about Alex's behavior, and in treating it as a group problem, I embraced the ideas of feminist pedagogy and encouraged the children's moral and academic learning.

We all agreed it pleased us to receive recognition for achieving the goals and behavior that led to learning. Hand clapping and praise occurred regularly, we kept charts with stickers, and I sent certificates and notes home. I agreed with the children that goals need to be different for each learner, so together, we set Alex's goals so he could achieve them. We talked about his need for physical space. I also got the children to realize that Alex had feelings too, and was sensitive, just as they were, to failure and ridicule. As the children became supportive and as understanding grew, Alex began to win applause, stickers, and certificates like the others. Slowly, we (and most of all Alex) saw his positive behavior at school increase. The change, of course, came slowly and with setbacks. Though he was not "cured" of his school difficulties, the changes we saw were for the most part in the right direction.

Discussion
Nevertheless, I found drawbacks to the models I followed or strategies I chose in my teaching. Each coin has two sides, and like a flipped coin, a choices implies something lost. Upon reflecting, I am increasingly convinced that giving something up—taking the risk of being different, trying something unconventional—is necessary to the natural evolution of teaching practice.

Spending so much time on social and moral growth in my classroom meant spending less time on actual writing and reading practice. Compared to other years, this class was at least a month "behind" learning the bank of sight words and phonic analyses they were "expected" to know in the first grade. I felt a constant struggle to balance my need to follow the established curriculum, with my even stronger need to follow the life curriculum my students brought to our classroom. With time so limited, I constantly looked for ways to integrate the former with the latter, in keeping with my belief that "learning must be relevant and connected to life experiences." I experienced the established curriculum as a constraint rather than an aid to introducing my students to language and story.

Life does not always feature an introduction followed by an activity, then a conclusion, as our linear curriculum would suggest. In real life, we have good days and bad days. Sometimes we deal with issues easily, other times we leave matters unresolved to be returned to after a break. With so much imposed "curriculum," I was challenged to preserve the natural individual pathways of my students' learning, and to capitalize on the potential of the group itself as a fund of knowledge and skill.

As a result, I found a good deal of relevance in Smyth's (1992) discussion of the paradox within the trend to make our schools more disciplined and our curricula more standardized (that is, controlled by centralized authority), while at the same time expecting schools to respond more autonomously to the needs and interests of diverse populations with more self-directedly reflective and collaborative teachers (that is, responsive to decentralized responsibility). Smyth described the "modernist" organization of schools as offering structured classes with linear and hierarchical curricula.

By contrast, and mirroring my own observations and frustrations, Schostak (1991) discussed a "postmodernist" vision in which learning is relevant to life and improves personhood, one's attitude toward oneself, and one's life experiences. Postmodernism embraces the idea that schooling change is upon us and that the organization and precepts of modernism are gradually crumbling:

> Education presents not packages of information to be transmitted, but the mechanisms, the principles and the procedures through which meetings and dialogues can take place (p. 25).

As I read these articles, I realized that the daily choices I made in my class to help Alex were small examples of this large evolution occurring in the way we define and relate to curricula and in the role we play as teachers. Schostak observed that

> The teacher, then, is professionally defined as one who enables relationships of teaching to take place rather than as under the old view, as one who is the sole source of teaching, a role carried out under conditions of compulsion. That is, the teacher opens the door to the everyday life experiences of others (p. 22).

This was the teacher I had hoped to be when I tried to see Alex as less a problem and more of a catalyst for my students to learn about life and about connections they could make with each other. This thinking failed to take the imposed curriculum I was expected to cover into account.

Related to the tension between constraints and openness in my teaching, an additional negative element surfaced in my observations: the absence of physical resources to create a more productive learning environment. It is frustrating to learn (and know) how to establish environments for optimum learning and then to be limited by sheer lack of space, desks, books, and storage. Today's Modernist Era schools still have linear, ordered classrooms with desks in organized patterns. Students move to ordered, time-limited classes through overcrowded halls that may have inadequate washroom facilities and lack lounge areas. Classrooms rarely come with different qualities of space, which we all need to learn at our best.

When I had group meetings with my students, we moved our desks which took teamwork and some problem solving, but also stole valuable minutes until we got settled and reorganized. Had we been able to adjourn to a nice meeting area, we may have had better transitions and possibly better meetings too. When Alex, or anyone needed a Time Out, we were so crowded it was hard to make the Time Out work the way it should. For example, because the Time Out desk was situated near the board at the front, anytime someone was in Time Out, we all had limited use of the chalkboard, which was often essential to the activity. I found this a continual annoyance and a problem I never did solve. While we continued to need a cooling off, isolation place in our room, I could find no suitable spot for it or for a child in need of quiet space.

If our schools offered more physical openness, we could use the space to pursue particular activities, rather than just to accommodate more and larger groups with places to sit. Rooms with platforms, podiums and small stages, and equipped with a collection of props and a variety of furniture, would be ideal for expressive activities. Students and teachers could act, meet, discuss, and read aloud. Other spaces might be reserved for solitary pursuits such as writing, reading, resting and thinking. Elsewhere, areas designed for listening and viewing could be provided. Teachers could reserve group time in various spaces, or individual students could use the areas up to certain density quotas and then be put on a call list. Spaces in the school building would ideally accommodate multi-age or skill groupings as well as specific age or skill groupings of students so as to help them learn comfortably. No doubt some of my frustrations in implementing the arrangements I chose for integrating Alex came from teaching with this postmodern vision in a resolutely modernist environment.

Some Closing Thoughts
I wish I could specify the magic that makes a great and memorable teacher. What my previous students recall most vividly tend to be tidbits that I have forgotten. They rarely mention what were memorable teaching moments for me. They remember that I had a "Joke of the Day" one April. A boy recalled how in third grade, to his relief, I taught him to tie his shoelaces. I read a particularly moving novel. I was often funny. It is hard to pinpoint a particular profile of an effective teacher from such a wide variety of random comments. Though I noticed his improved behavior and interest in learning, I cannot tell if I have deeply touched Alex or any of his classmates, or if they will have lasting memories of learning with me.

I can, however, be certain that reflecting on my own teaching and addressing a particularly stressful situation in my practice all the while considering current educational paradigms has helped me gain insight into my students, has encouraged me to keep teaching "on the threshold," and has validated the experience of writing and reflecting I have undertaken. By reading, writing, and talking about current educational thought with colleagues, I continue to develop an informed context and a sense of community in which my own teaching practice can evolve.

References

Avery, C. (1990). Learning to research/ researching to learn. In M. Olson (ed.), *Opening the door to classroom research*. Newark, Delaware: International Reading Association.

Edelsky, C., Draper, K., & Smith, K. (1983). Hookin' 'em at the start of school in a "whole language" classroom. *Anthropology & Education Quarterly, 14*, 257-281.

Elliott, J. (1987). Teachers as researchers. In M. Dunkin (ed.), *International encyclopedia of teaching and teacher education* (pp. 162-164). New York: Pergamon Press.

Henderson, J.G. (1992). *Reflective teaching: Becoming an inquiring educator*. New York: Macmillan.

Lieberman A. (Ed.). (1990). *Schools as collaborative cultures: Creating the future now*. New York: Falmer Press.

McConaghy, J. (1990). *Children learning through literature: A teacher researcher study*. New Hampshire: Heinemann Educational Books.

Noddings, N. (1988). An ethic of caring and its implications for instructional arrangements. *American Journal of Education,* February, 215-230.

Paley, V.G. (1986). On listening to what children say. *Harvard Educational Review. 56* (2), 122-131.

Schostak, J. (1991). Modernism, post-modernism and the curriculum of surfaces. Paper presented at the first Invitational Symposium on Teacher Education. Spencer Hall, University of Western Ontario.

Sergiovanni, T.J. (1994). *Building community in schools*. San Fransisco: Jossey-Bass.

Shrewsbury, C. (1987). What is feminist pedagogy? *Women's Studies Quarterly, 15* (3&4), 6-14.

Shute, R.W. and Gibb, S. (1993). *Students of thought.* Alberta: Detselig Enterprises.

Smyth, J. (1992). Teachers' work and the politics of reflection. *American Educational Research Journal, 29* (2), 267-300.

White, C. (1990). *Jevon doesn't sit at the back anymore.* Toronto: Scholastic.

Chapter Six

Joanna Learns to Read

Kathy Nawrot

The ability to read precedes and affects all of a child's subsequent academic achievements. If the reading foundation is solid, the child can proceed to lay bricks of success one upon another, building a stronger edifice. If the foundation is absent or weak, the structure sways and probably topples.

As an elementary school teacher, I continually met students with serious reading difficulties who had been left behind as their peers developed the routine skills and went on to new challenges and achievements. These children worried me because they could not keep up with their peers and the grade requirements, and they failed to master the new skills and concepts others were being taught. They seemed to have entered a circle of frustration that offered no way out.

Out of concern for these children and a desire to help them break out of this cycle, I began to search for ways to help them overcome their reading difficulties. Finding my own knowledge and experimenting inadequate for this goal, I turned for assistance to formal education, and what my studies taught me changed my thinking about learning to read.

Emergent Literacy

Educators once considered learning to read a process most children navigated as a result of instruction, usually by a first grade teacher but occasionally by a parent or sibling. If a child received that instruction when he or she was ready, the child usually learned to read. Reading readiness involved a number of variables including attention span, memory and hand-eye coordination. If a child failed to learn to read, a lack of readiness was often assumed to be the cause. This belief, of course, had implications for the way reading problems were remediated.

Educators now believe, however, that a child sets in motion the process of learning to read long before entering school and beginning formal instruction. Smith observed that "children probably begin to read from the moment they become aware of print in a meaningful way, and. . . the roots of reading are discernible whenever children strive to make sense of print, before they are able to recognize many of the actual words" (as cited in Doake, 1981, p. 102).

This belief in emergent literacy assumes that literacy is more than just decoding the words on a page of text. It involves using written language in meaningful ways, and it recognizes that the idea of text extends beyond combinations of 26 letters.

As I considered this view of emergent literacy, I became aware of examples around me in which young children exhibited reading and writing behaviors. Pre-schoolers can identify the McDonalds restaurants even in unfamiliar cities. They can pick out the cereal box they want in the grocery store. They can distinguish between a library book and a coloring book. The more I observed, the more I became convinced that this view of emergent literacy promised to describe literacy as it really is.

The gradual process of learning to read begins early in life when children see print and see their parents using it. Children soon engage in the reading-like behaviors they see others modeling around them. Children progress in their journey through literacy at vastly different rates and along different pathways, but by the time they begin formal reading instruction in school, they have all made some progress.

My Need to Research
With only this general view in mind, I realized how little I knew about the process of learning to read. I then began to wonder how I could help children with only a limited conception of how they actually do learn to read. I saw that I needed a better basis for my reading remediation lessons than just a knowledge of how to diagnose specific reading problems and a list of strategies for correcting them. I needed a framework

for my knowledge of literacy, and I needed more than just a set of theories. I had to see the theories in action to understand in practice what I read on paper.

In short, I was ready to conduct my own research into the question of how children learn to read. Knowing that my entry question was much too broad, I decided to focus on a single subject case study: my niece, Joanna.

Merriam (1988) suggested that we "use a case study design in order to gain an in-depth understanding of the situation and its meaning for those involved. The interest is in process rather than outcomes, in context rather than a specific variable, in discovery rather than confirmation" (1988, p.xii). She also asserted that it is "often the best methodology for addressing. . . problems in which understanding is sought in order to improve practice [and that] by concentrating on a single phenomenon or entity, this approach aims to uncover the interaction of significant factors characteristic of the phenomenon" (pp. xii, xiii, 10).

The Research Procedure
Joanna had just turned four when I began my study. I visited her and her family regularly—weekly when possible—and usually spent time alone with Joanna and her one year-old sister. I often brought library books with me and Joanna came to expect that I would offer books to read to her. In fact, she commented to me once, "Kath, you like to read a lot, don't you?"

Joanna and I read books together, both the ones I brought and ones she owned. As she got older, her sister joined us for longer and longer periods. We also played together, often acting out scenes with Joanna's dolls. Throughout our time together I was alert for manifestations of literacy and sometimes questioned her further or steered the conversation in a desired direction, recording the conversations on tape. After each visit I wrote down my observations and transcribed the tapes. Between visits I reread what I had written and composed reflections on what I had seen and how it pertained to theory I had studied. At the same time, Joanna's mother also looked for signs of literacy and related them to me. She saved samples of Joanna's written work and gave them to me along with a description of the context out of which each came. In keeping with the principles of qualitative research, I conducted my observations in a natural setting, usually in Joanna's home, and I became a participant-observer. This arrangement allowed me to view and record the behaviors Joanna engaged in. I could ask my questions and steer conversations and pretend play into promising directions. As Bogdan and Biklen (1992) suggested, participant-observation interviews tend to become more like conversations and difficult to separate from other research activities. In fact, Joanna's age made formal interviews difficult. Conversations mixed with play were much more productive. Interviews with Joanna's mother entailed informal conversations in which she would describe what she had observed and I would question her about what I had observed that puzzled me.

Thus, I describe here an interpretive inquiry using participant-observation as the primary research activity. I approached the research without any clear questions or specific directions to follow. I knew only that I needed to learn more about the process of learning to read and that a more practical understanding of the process would probably help me remediate my students' reading problems.

The Progression of the Research

Bogdan and Biklen (1992) observed that a qualitative researcher does not assume that he or she knows enough to identify the important concern at the beginning of a study. Rather, he or she uses a part of the study to learn what the important questions are. Merriam (1988) has also insisted that "the focus must be allowed to emerge and in fact may change over the course of the study" (p. 87).

I found myself agreeing with Bogdan and Biklen and with Merriam. I began my study thinking that I would proceed linearly, testing Joanna's knowledge of print to establish a standard and then simply watching as she reached new levels of reading and text awareness. I intended to test periodically to ascertain her progress. In other words, I expected to discover a progression of skills and levels as she became more proficient.

Instead, I discovered a wealth of information about Joanna's flirtations with literacy—not a dry list of skills and levels of development—but stories and discoveries all tied to contextual and social situations. I began to be led in new directions, and with each observation, I found myself asking new questions. After a year of study, I was no longer interested in testing Joanna's level of development.

I also found that I changed my stance as the year progressed. I began by seeing myself as an observer-as-participant. I saw my role as primarily a researcher intending to record what Joanna was doing. Before long, however, Joanna had drawn me into her world, sharing her books and requiring that I play with her dolls. I became a participant-as-observer as our relationship took center stage in the research.

As the year progressed, I became better at writing field notes that included thick descriptions. I also began to add reflections, and in composing those reflections, I discovered definite themes running through my observations.

The data that formed the basis for my interpretive inquiry consisted of field notes describing the observations I made, including comments about nonverbal behavior; transcripts of conversations between Joanna and me; transcripts of information supplied by Joanna's mother; the notes about observations Joanna's mother wrote; and samples of Joanna's writing.

Concerns About the Research

The interpretations I derived from my study raise three important issues. The first issue centers on the fact that I was observing a child closely related to me. I expected this to cause some bias on my part, both in what I chose to record and in the way I interpreted my observations. The possibility of bias may, however, be eclipsed by a major advantage: my association with the family provided me with access to information about and understanding of the context of what I observed.

A second issue centers on the effect of my role on Joanna's literacy growth. It is impossible to became a participant-observer without influencing the behavior being observed. By bringing books into her house and reading regularly to Joanna, I directly influenced her growth. Even though I tried to limit my involvement to simply reading, questioning and observing, my very interest in her literacy must have affected her development and attitude. But since I could hardly change this effect, in order to maintain an adequate portrayal of how a child learns to read, I tried to do no more than an interested mother would do to affect her child's learning.

A third issue centers on the difficulty of making generalizations based upon a study of one child. Certainly the paths to literacy other children follow resemble Joanna's, but many more follow very different routes. I was studying only what Merriam called a "slice of life" and could not presume that this slice represented the whole. In fact, I chose to examine theories of literacy learning while observing Joanna, specifically hoping that the practical observations would illustrate or clarify aspects of the theoretical models.

Moreover, I could avoid some of the problems with generalization by producing thorough descriptions of my observations that would allow readers to base their conclusions on their own experiences. As McCutcheon (1991) noted, "Generalizability rests on the assumption of the intersubjectivity of interpretation and the readers' ability to generalize personally to their own situations rather than on the researcher's generalizing to populations larger than the sample used" (p. 9).

Analyzing the Data

My study of Joanna's path to literacy divides itself naturally into three sections: the first year at age four in which the major influence in her life was her home; the second year at age five in which the influence of kindergarten would be introduced; and the third year at age six which would be influenced by grade one. At the end of the first year, before Joanna began kindergarten, I thought it would be useful to stop and analyze the data that first year of observation had produced.

Understanding interpretive inquiry within the discourse hermeneutics offers, I recognized that my fore-structure had predisposed me to find certain themes emerging. I recorded these and then returned to my data to find instances of the themes and to identify how they appeared in Joanna's learning. This step is the forward arc of the hermeneutic circle described in Chapter 2.

But the hermeneutic circle also requires a backward arc, a questioning of the interpretation and an analysis of the data designed to uncover inconsistencies, gaps and omissions. As I reread my notes, I placed each event in the appropriate theme and discovered new themes of which I had been unaware. As I examined the material I had placed within each theme, I noticed that Joanna's understandings in some areas were far more extensive than I had realized and that some of the themes I had expected to be important appeared to play a more limited role.

Literacy Behaviors as a Theme

During the year I looked specifically for the literacy behaviors Joanna engaged in without adult direction. I believed that this orientation would yield information about both the extent of her literacy skills and her attitude toward literacy. I looked for both because research on emergent literacy suggests that reading and writing are interwoven (Doake, 1981; Harste, Woodward and Burke, 1984).

Joanna lives in a literacy-rich environment. Both parents are professional people and she often sees them engaged in reading and writing. Her mother has chosen to stay at home with her children and believes strongly in reasoning and explaining. Joanna's vocabulary shows evidence of many such conversations.

Joanna herself owns many books, all easily accessible. She keeps some in her bedroom, and others are with her toys. She has her own magazine subscription and she looks at her mother's magazines and catalogues. She has access to paper, scissors, crayons, tape, stapler, pencils and pens, and she does not usually require permission to use them.

Watching Joanna, I expected to see instances in which she copied the literacy behavior of adults. After listing the examples when this occurred, I began to wonder why a child would choose to copy adult behavior. I knew that children learn to copy their parents' speech in learning to talk, but one of the prime reasons for doing so is to get what they want. In a sense, they learn to control their worlds through speech. I reasoned that children must also recognize that the reading and writing their parents do gives them additional power and control.

Accordingly, many of Joanna's literacy behaviors seemed to help her attain some control of her world. She was often read to by both her parents and me and in those situations, we readers maintained the power. But Joanna's mother once came upon Joanna with her dolls all lined up while she "read" them a story. She also "read" stories to her little sister and even added explanations to help her sister understand. She placed herself in the more powerful position of the reader, even usurping additional power by explaining as well as reading.

She both "read" books to others and created them. In one instance, she used an empty date book, added "writing" to each square, and then "read" the book back to her sister. On other occasions, she wrote or drew on serviettes and stapled them together into books. She also put animal cards into a photo album which she then read to her sister.

One night I noticed Joanna had arranged her books into a library. Another night she had created a bookstore for me to visit and buy books. These activities changed the power between us; she became the book owner and I became the user.

Her desire to control part of her world proceeded further when she used literacy to help her interact with others. After her first hair cut she wrote "notes" to three girls in playschool to tell them about her adventure. Another day she made up birthday cards and valentines. As she became more adept at printing letters, she began to leave messages around the house. Many nights her parents discovered her notes on the top of the stairs for them to find as they went to bed. One such note, printed on Kleenex, contained the names of family members and her doll. Another, also on Kleenex, had pictures of characters labeled with their names and drawn to retell a story Joanna and her mother had read.

As her fifth birthday approached, Joanna attempted to use literacy to exert even more control. She made lists of the initials of people she planned to invite to her party. She wrote out portions of her birthday invitations. Then she presented her mother with a recipe card detailing the food she wanted for her party.

Reading Strategies as a Theme
In addition to collecting the literacy behaviors Joanna exhibited, I looked for data that would help me understand her concept of reading. This data emerged much as my forestructure had led me to anticipate. She began the year by acknowledging that she did not know how to read by herself, but she could use the pictures to explain what the book was about. She knew what a book was for, in what direction to turn the pages, and on which page the story began. She knew the difference between typed words and pictures, and she recognized that the words were to be read.

Theories involving emergent literacy specify a child's recognition of environmental print as a powerful argument that children enter into literacy at a very young age. At four, Joanna was already adept at reading environmental print. She could name the stores she saw. She could even identify which store had produced a certain brochure. She could choose the correct cereal box in the cupboard and knew that the cardboard carton in the fridge said "milk."

As I contemplated the data from my first year of observations, I began to wonder what it was about environmental print that encouraged and allowed Joanna to read it. To find out, I printed the word "McDonalds" and asked Joanna what it said. She didn't know. Then I printed "McDonalds" again using the logo arches in place of the "M." Immediately she read it correctly. She had required the logo arches to read the word.

Joanna's mother told me that Joanna had learned the word "exit" at playschool. It had apparently been "drilled into the children," and her mother said Joanna pointed it out any time she saw it. I wrote the word "exit" on my paper and Joanna could not read it. But, when I read it to her, she was able to describe its meaning and use on signs.

While I was pondering these discoveries, I came upon an article by Harste, Woodward and Burke (1984) reporting that children use the same reading strategies as adults. I began to consider this idea and came to the conclusion that Joanna's reading of environmental print represented an application of two adult reading strategies. The first was the use of context to predict words. Proficient readers use this strategy to allow them to read quickly and fluently. Joanna read store names where she expected to read store names. She read "milk" because she knew from experience that containers of that shape and color stored in the fridge contain milk. She read "exit" when she saw the appropriate sign above the door, but not when she saw it on paper where she had not expected it.

Her second strategy for reading environmental print was to look at the shape of the word. Few proficient readers take the time to check all the letters in a word. If they know what words they expect to see, they can confirm their predictions by the general shape of the words: tall letters, hanging letters, many or few letters. Joanna had recognized "McDonalds" by the distinctive color and shape of its "M."

Comprehension Strategies as a Theme

My research into emergent literacy had also prepared me to expect that children seek meaning in their world (Haussler, 1985; Waring-Chaffee, 1994). Consequently, while reading to Joanna, I had been alert for instances when she had sought meaning from the story. I was not disappointed. I discovered that the meaning of the story held a great deal of importance for her.

As I considered Joanna's use of reading strategies to *read* environmental print, I realized that she was also using proficient reader strategies to *comprehend* the material she read. But, she was applying the strategies to listening instead of reading. This revelation sent me back to my data to identify the specific strategies she adopted.

As one example, I found she used the picture on the cover to predict what would happen in the story. Occasionally she would sit and leaf through the entire book before bringing it to me to read. Also, before allowing me to start, she often asked for the name of the book. She made inferences from the pictures and used information from the pictures to answer the "why" questions I sometimes asked. She identified the pictures of the characters as the book introduced them. When the characters confused her, she asked me to identify their pictures.

She made suggestions for solving a character's dilemma and then took notice of whether her suggestion was right. She made inferences on the basis of her background knowledge, and when she became aware that her knowledge was inadequate, she asked questions instead. Her comments and inferences were not always accurate, but they were based logically on her experience and knowledge.

Usually Joanna sat quietly through the first reading of a book unless the story really excited her, confused her or reflected her own experience. Often, however, she requested multiple readings of the same book, and on the second and subsequent readings, she interrupted to offer explanations or repeat the comments that I had made during the first reading.

As proficient readers do, she also extended her understanding beyond the book. She had dolls of many of the characters in her books, and she re-enacted parts of the stories or made up new ones, being careful to remain true to the characters themselves. When she used Tigger (from *The House at Pooh Corner* by A. A. Milne) during one of our pretend games, she made him hop across the room and then commented, "Because that's what Tiggers do best," a phrase right out of the book.

The fact that Joanna had already developed and used a number of comprehension strategies while listening to stories made me wonder about the process of comprehension. To comprehend a story, whether as a result of listening or reading, we must take a concrete piece of text and make it abstract within our understanding. As proficient readers and listeners, we often use an intermediate symbolic step: we form an image in our minds. Perhaps this is the real value of using picture books for beginning readers. It gives them that symbolic representation for the story.

Names as a Theme
Joanna demonstrated far more advanced literacy understandings than I expected, particularly in her command over the same reading and comprehension strategies proficient readers use. But as I followed her progress in the identification

and use of letters as a literacy strategy, I found yet another surprise.

Almost all of the important steps she made toward the actual decoding of words were directly connected to names— her own first, then the names of family, friends and important fictional characters. This association began, I believe, at a very early age when her mother encouraged her to add her name to the family's letters, Christmas cards and birthday cards. At first, she signed a series of up and down wavy lines. Then she learned to print the letters of her name and began to recognize those same letters in other writing. She learned the names of the rest of her family and friends at playschool, and eventually she began naming all her dolls and stuffed animals. She became fascinated with identifying which letters began specific names and initiated a game with her mother whereby she said, "I'm thinking of a name that starts with _____."

Soon she realized that other names besides hers began with "J" and so discovered she had to look at more than just the first letter. Eventually she began to recognize some sounds, but always based on the letters in names and the similarities between names.

Names gave Joanna a reason for writing. She made up lists of party-goers and wrote labels under pictures. Just as children who are beginning to speak learn the words for the most meaningful items in their world, so in learning to read and write, Joanna began with the most meaningful words in her own world—her name and the names of the people who are most important to her.

Future Directions

The research described here continues. In one sense, it has another two years before I will be content to stop and formally evaluate what I have learned. This first year of study provided a rich source of information about the beginnings of literacy, but it also left me with many questions, some of which will direct my future research. For example, what will be the effect of formal schooling on Joanna's self-directed quest for literacy? As she learns to read text, what strategies will become most important to her? How will she integrate the strategies she already has as she learns to decode words?

In fact, this research will continue much further. The understanding I gain will remain with me and I will continue to reflect and question long after I complete the project. Every new idea, every new revelation, will be just one more step along the path.

Implications of the Research

Nevertheless, the research reported here has already affected my teaching and colored the way I approach the reading problems my students present. I recognize in a way I have never fully recognized before, that most valuable learning is self-directed. I find myself allowing students more freedom than I have ever granted. I supply the materials and encouragement, I am the interested and enthusiastic audience, but I recognize that they are the learners and they have much to teach themselves and each other.

I also recognize the power of listening to stories as a means for developing those hard-to-teach comprehension skills. I now consider the time to have been well spent when we read and discuss a story together.

I have also discovered a powerful resource to teach decoding, sound-symbol correspondence and spelling skills: the students' own names. Now I look here first for an example and find it is the example my students remember best. A student who notices his or her own name in a piece of writing has a powerful motivator to read.

One can take many different pathways to literacy and children do not all follow the same sequence of steps. While I want to avoid generalizing Joanna's adventure to all children, I can say, "This is how it happened for one child." In some cases, what I saw Joanna do confirmed what theorists had predicted. In other cases, what she did was uniquely individual and not applicable to other children's experiences. But sharing her adventure has given me a basic framework that now helps me make sense of the experiences of other children and even helps me see where I can assist some of the children who are struggling.

References

Bogdan, R.C. & Biklen, S.K. (1992). *Qualitative research for education: An introduction to theory and methods.* Boston: Allyn and Bacon.

Denzin, N.K. & Lincoln, Y.S. (1994). Introduction: Entering the field of qualitative research. In N.K. Denzin and Y.S. Lincoln (eds.), *Handbook of qualitative research* (pp. 1-17). Thousand Oaks, CA: Sage Publications.

Doake, D.B. (1981). Book experience and emergent reading behavior in preschool children. Unpublished doctoral dissertation, University of Alberta.

Harste, J.C., Woodward, V.A., & Burke, C.L. (1984). *Language stories and literacy lessons.* Portsmouth, NH: Heinemann Educational Books.

Haussler, M.M. (1985). A young child's developing concepts of print. In A. Jaggar, and M.T. Smith-Burke (eds.), *Observing the language learner.* Urbana, IL: International Reading Association and National Council of Teachers.

McCutcheon, G. (1981). On the interpretatlon of classroom observations. *Educational Researcher,* May, 5-10.

Merriam, S. (1988). *Case study research in education: A qualitative approach.* San Francisco: Jossey Bass Publishers.

Waring-Chaffee, M.B. (1994). RDRNOT...HRIKM (Ready or Not, Here I Come!): Investigations in children's emergence as readers and writers. *Young Children, 49*(6), 52-55.

Chapter Seven

The Role of Student-Teacher Dialogue Journals in Building Language and Establishing Community

Judith McIntyre

> O, the comfort, the inexpressible comfort of feeling safe with a person, neither having to weigh thoughts nor measure words, but pouring them right out just as they are, chaff and grain alike; certain that a faithful hand will take and sift them, keep what is worth keeping and then with the breath of kindness, blow the rest away.
>
> —George Eliot
> *Middlemarch* (1874)

Introductory Stories of Belonging

"I'm yours, aren't I? I'm really in the third grade? My name is on the door and everything?" I smiled back at Darren. The year so far had been difficult for both of us. Often excluded from activities because of his difficulties with academic tasks, Darren had struggled with loneliness. We had just returned from a field trip and Darren's inclusion on the trip meant that he belonged and had been accepted in my room. I, myself, had returned from a year's sabbatical and was feeling frustrated at trying to assimilate newly embraced theoretical perspectives and teaching practices into an environment which treated change as an unnecessary evil. I did not feel that I exactly belonged and I could identify with Darren's feelings.

The need for me to feel that I fit in was hardly new, as a memory of my first grade education recorded much later illustrates:

The first grade classroom resembled many classrooms of the time. The wooden desks were placed in long rows that faced front. The teacher's desk was in the front corner beside the long row of windows. Above the blackboard was the alphabet: A is for Apple, B is for Ball, C is for Cat. Pictures of the Queen and the Union Jack graced the front wall. The shelves below the windows contained the instruction books. Everything was neat and orderly, including the display of pictures on the back bulletin board. This room could be distinguished from the others in the school only by the size of its desks. I sat in one of these desks, my hand raised high, my other hand clutching my pencil. "Pick up your pencil and hold it up" the teacher instructed. Automatically I grabbed the fat red pencil with my left hand and waved it proudly. I quickly switched my pencil to my right hand when I noticed that the right-handed children received smiles and the rest were told to change hands. Now I too would earn a smile for holding my pencil in the correct hand, the right hand. "This is the hand you will learn to print with," continued the teacher. Even though I had been in school for only a few days, I knew it was important to follow instructions and win the teacher's smiles. I already felt the "power" she had over me. Up until this point, I had always grasped first with my left hand. But from this time on, I would use the right because it was the one the teacher approved of. In my mind, "belonging" meant being right-handed.

Over the years the children in my classrooms have also, in their own ways, expressed the need to feel that they belong and to establish their places in the classroom. None, however, have done it with such insistence as third grade Elissa exhibited in her journal.

Day One

Elissa: I like Melanie, Janel, and Daniel.
             I like dogs.
             I like you. Do you like me?

Teacher: I'm really glad to have you in my class.

Day Two

Elissa: But do YOU like ME!!!?
            Answer YES or NO
            Check one.
            Yes_____ No_____

Teacher: (I checked off Yes with a bright red pen.)
            Yes, I like you.

Day Three

Elissa: Just checking!

This powerful exchange reminded me of my own much earlier desire to belong. Elissa sought affirmation that she was a valuable member of the class and that she had the teacher's approval. She used her journal to reveal a personal need she could not express orally. The journal gave her a chance to engage a companion who (once I realized what she wanted) could provide her with the support she needed. The journal entries were neither sophisticated nor indicative of much academic learning. Elissa was not trying to write creatively, nor was she overly concerned with the mechanics of writing. She wrote to express a need; she had to know that she belonged.

The worlds of the children in my classroom are often unfamiliar. Their lives outside of school seem far more complicated than mine was at their age. My childhood experiences were mainly positive and my family provided me with a secure learning environment. In my classroom, I want to provide that caring, productive environment—a place where children feel safe taking risks. Such a place accommodates their different needs and produces answers to their questions about the world. To provide it, I must find a way to enter the world of my students and see through their eyes. I must accept them where they are, for who they are at this point. I want my classroom to be a place where children like Elissa can freely ask their questions and receive honest answers.

My Question

How can teachers like me develop relationships with their students so as to respect and honor the knowledge those children already have and can build upon? My journal exchange with Elissa allowed me to enter briefly into such a relationship. Elissa used her journal to seek affirmation, to share thoughts and ideas, and to ask questions. My responses showed that I wanted to understand her better and learn what it was like in her world. Might the use of dialogue journals provide teachers with an entrance into caring relationships with children? van Manen (1986) called such a relationship one of "thoughtfulness, sustained by a certain kind of seeing, of listening, of responding," and also observed that

> How and what we see depends on who and what we are in the world. How and what we see in a child is dependent on our relationship to that child (pp. 12, 16).

I decided to study the relationships children and teachers can achieve through their dialogue journal writing.

Classroom Journals

I began my inquiry by examining journal entries and responses taken from a fourth grade and a sixth grade classroom. Each teacher provided me with the journals of eight or ten children randomly selected, a mixture of boys and girls. They had written their entries during language arts classes, and journals were a required element in these programs. While the journals went ungraded, participation was not optional.

Philip's Class

Philip collected the journals from his fourth grade classroom each Monday, and he responded to them that same day. The format in each journal remained the same every week. The students' entries focused on retelling their weekend activities; the responses consisted of short comments.

As I read the entries I was often struck by a feeling of empathetic frustration. The children had submitted lengthy entries sharing their weekend adventures but generally received only such "generic" comments as "Sounds like an interesting weekend." Philip made no other marks and his comments seemed so routinized I wondered if he had really read the entries. One child obviously wanted to share an item with his class and his teacher :

> Tony gave me a mixie [a kind of marble]. It is a really shiny one. It looks brand new today. I hope I can show it to you at our show and tell time.

But Philip made no response. Had this child been as disappointed as I, a second hand reader, was? Would he volunteer to share again? In fact, I could find no suggestions that the children themselves ever read the comments Philip made about their entries. There seemed little reason for them to reread their entries and respond to other comments.

I noticed that none of the entries addressed anyone in particular; names were rarely mentioned in the journal entries or teacher comments. The entries mainly listed off activities chronologically with little personal information or emotion expressed by either the children or their teacher. I must say I found it difficult to make a personal connection with the writers who shared "little of substance." The entries were hardly dialogues between two people. Philip's comment regarding acceptable length—"Next time you have to write 2 pages,"—indicated that he used these journals as a "busy work" to fill time. He emphasized quantity over quality. Later he told me that his students wrote their entries only once a week because the activity took too much time and responding more frequently would be burdensome.

Fulwiler (1987), Staton (1988a), and Hall (1994), all discussed various interactions that can be part of journal writing. I myself, view journal writing as a conversation between two interested participants but obviously saw little evidence of this view in the entries from Philip's classroom. Neither party showed much enthusiasm for the activity, and Philip provided little encouragement to initiate dialogues. These journals were less "a responsive form of writing in which the student and teacher carry on a conversation over time, sharing ideas, feelings, and concerns in writing" than "shopping lists" of events that received cursory replies (Staton, 1987, p. 47). I hoped to see a teacher using journal writing to respond to his students. As Staton (1987) observed, "We reply to questions; we respond to persons" (p. 47). A response like this involves a commitment of self, an engagement with the other, a sharing of oneself, and Philip appeared to be avoiding this commitment.

Donna's Class
The second group of journals, taken from Donna's sixth grade classroom, more closely reflected Staton's ideal response. The entry formats varied from person to person, but most of the students used a friendly letter format, addressing their teacher personally and signing their names. Donna responded in kind. The children addressed their teacher as "Mrs. T," which indicated to me that teacher and students felt comfortable addressing each other informally. Moreover, the entries appeared to be written as a need to communicate arose, not on a predetermined schedule.

Both parties shared personal information in their writing. They discussed their feelings and emotions, asked questions, sought validation. In the following entry, Tyler apologizes for discussing his success in soccer.

> Tyler: P. S. Sorry if I'm bragging.
>
> Teacher: Congratulations! I don't think you are brag-
>   ging at all. It feels good to do well, and telling
>   someone in this way is not bragging.

Tyler also feels free to confide that he sometimes feels less successful in his studies; Donna replies that she thinks this year will be different. She responds to an inquiry about her weekend activities by relating a recent adventure. She also shares information about her family. Karen's story of a recent trip invites her teacher to share a pleasant, validating memory:

> Teacher: You know I remember when you first began
>   dancing! You were so excited.

I thoroughly enjoyed reading these entries, mainly because they taught me much about both teacher and students. They freely shared something of themselves with each other, and all parties seemed to enjoy "talking" to each other and welcomed the opportunity to correspond. The journal entries opened the world the sixth graders experienced and it became clearer to me. The writing focused on the ideas they wished to communicate, not on the form the sharing should take. The teacher's responses centered on the content. I could see many instances where both students and teacher had reread previous entries and resumed a conversation from a previous entry. As I read the entries and responses I sensed that this teacher and her children "saw " each other. As van Manen (1986) wrote,

> Being seen is more than being acknowledged. For a child it means experiencing being seen by the teacher. It means being confirmed as existing, as being a person and a learner (p. 21).

In Donna's responses I could sense a comfort in their mutual relationships—a sense of place and the sense of belonging I sought to achieve. But was this feeling a result of something else entirely out of sight that had gone on in the classroom or simply of the journal writing experiences? Might it represent some kind of interaction between the two?

Surveying Teachers and Children

Rereading the journal entries and the teacher responses from the two classes, I found many of my prior assumptions about journalling confirmed. The writing varied from child to child, some more at home with the written word and with storytelling than others. I resolved to resist a single "standard" for journal writing. Formats vary among teachers and among children, and they should. A productive dialogue takes place when each participant rereads and responds to what has gone before.

I was surprised in Philip's case by the infrequency of the journals two months into the school term. I saw little evidence of students and teacher rereading previous entries. I was disappointed by Philip's "generic" replies to many entries. I found little evidence of either the teacher of his students engaged in reflective thinking in the entries. These observations raised new questions, and I had to "back up" and examine the reasons why teachers use journals in the first place.

The most important reason for using journals, I had always assumed, was to help children find meaning in their worlds—that is, as a way of gaining both academic and personal understanding. A journal is a personal communication between two interested parties. But how did the two teachers who shared their journals with me see their role in the exercise? How did they structure the activity? What did their students think about the responses they received? I hoped that answers to these questions would help me use journals to create caring relationships in my own classroom.

I asked Donna, Philip and some of their randomly selected students some general questions about the use of journals. Then I asked the same questions of other teachers and children who used journals in their classroom activities. I asked these four key questions:

1. Why do you use journals?

2. Do you respond? How?

3. Do journals tell you anything?

4. What do you think journals should be used for?

I found I could classify the comments teachers offered into two general categories: views of journalling as an academically based writing activity; and views of journals as a place for conversations, a way of communicating with others.

Journalling as Academic Writing
This group of teachers saw journals as a part of the language arts curriculum. They described journal entries as opportunities for children to write about favorite books, practice creative writing, and improve such written communication skills as punctuation and spelling. Journal writing, for them, was a structured activity, often taking place once a week, with clear expectations regarding length and format. Responding to children's entries meant saying something positive or

nothing at all. Some teachers indicated that they occasionally questioned a child orally about his or her entries to gain understanding. Others commented on the mechanics of the writing as they used journal entries to judge growth in spelling and writing: "I look for improvement every week;" and "They should be better every time."

As I read the answers the teachers wrote in response to my questions, I wondered if they saw journal writing as an "unnecessary evil" imposed only because they felt they should. Perhaps for them journal writing duplicated other writing activities perceived as more useful and effective.

Journalling as Communication
The other group of teachers spoke about the use of journals as a way of encouraging children to communicate. They described journals as places for children to share personal information: "It's a safe place for them to write to me about anything they wish to;" "They tell me about what they like to do;" and "They talk about the weekend."

These teachers placed less emphasis on the mechanics, focusing instead on what was being said. They responded by asking questions in the hope of starting and maintaining a dialogue. They responded in full sentences instead of words. The children's entries were not always restricted to assigned topics and the frequency of writing varied. The students made journal entries whenever they felt the need to communicate about an area of interest. Their teachers saw journals as a way to get to know their students, and it appeared that these teachers enjoyed reading the journal entries.

The Students' Voices
I also talked to students involved in journal writing and asked them to enter into a discussion with me by completing the following three phrases:

1. In my journal . . .

2. I think journals are . . .

3. Teachers . . .

The messages I received about their view of journal writing revealed that the students welcomed the opportunity to "talk" to their teachers about what was important to them. They said they wrote about their activities, dreams and discoveries. They expressed indignation at those times when a direct question went unanswered or when they had to write more than they had to say in order to fill a quota imposed by the teacher. Some comments reveal that for many children one of the most important parts of the journal was the interchange of ideas and thoughts between the participants: "You should write me back and say nice stuff and tell me secrets because I told you one;" and "I liked it when you write me stuff back and tell me your things."

I also observed my own primary class as they wrote, read, and reread their journal entries. I noticed that when I passed their journals back, they immediately checked for what I had written. Faces fell if I had neglected to add a personal observation or comment.

Both groups of teachers focused upon what the children were writing and perceived their own responses as less important. Their responses to my questions focused on encouraging children to communicate information to the teacher, with little mention of teachers communicating and sharing with students. Neither group mentioned what their roles as teachers were in the journal writing process. Teachers talked about wanting their students to respond to ideas and questions and to relate personal information while writing more and improving their skills. But had that message been communicated in the responses they made to the journal entries?

How Conversations Work
When I talk to a friend, I enter into the conversation expecting that he or she will acknowledge and respond to my topic before bringing up a new one; try to add new and relevant information; be honest; and try to avoid trite comments. I expect a good friend to be a good listener. If the responses I receive are "Mmm hmm," "That's nice, dear" or "You should use 'whom' not 'who'," then I am unlikely to proceed much further. I will relate only what I have to, perceiving that my listener cares little about what I have to say. If my

friend ignores my message and indicates that his or her topic is more important than mine, I will reveal little. The same "rules" apply to the responses to journal conversations. As van Manen (1986) noted,

> An appropriate answer for a particular child is a story that belongs to that child. A good story provides an answer that remembers the child's interest in questioning. A tactful educator will keep alive the interest that produced the child's question (p. 41).

What words do we use to encourage conversation and to keep alive that child's interest in the question? Are the words the same for oral and written dialogue? What do teachers say that tells children that they are interested and want to know more?

A quick brainstorming session with a colleague produced a list of useful words and phrases: share, explore, tell me more, what about, have you thought about, why do you think, could it be, discuss, tell, would you like. Scanning the teacher responses in my original journal collection, I saw the teachers used few of these formulas as they responded to their students' entries. Yet those same teachers orally expressed dissatisfaction with the writing the children produced in their journals: "Their writing doesn't tell me anything interesting;" and "I wish they would build upon what they already have said."

The teachers used words and phrases like "Good work!" "Nice" and "Interesting weekend!" Such comments convey little encouragement for the children to expand upon their original writing. Nor did the comments indicate what the teacher considered good or nice about the work or interesting about the weekend. In his article, "Do Teachers Communicate with Their Students as if They Were Dogs?" Madden (1988) discussed how statements of praise can be changed to statements of encouragement by recognizing the contribution or some growth in behavior and refraining from making judgments about the students as a result of their behavior. The title of the article gave me pause. Could there be a resemblance between how we talk to our pets and the glib comments teachers so often make: "Good girl" or "Nice try" or "Way to go"?

Sara Joins My Inquiry

I invited my colleague Sara to help with my research after hearing her concerns over the journal writing in her classroom. She expressed an interest in exploring the topic of journals and how she might modify her current practices to make journal writing more effective.

In her fifth grade class, Sara assigns journal writing once a week, on Monday mornings. Her students write for about 15 minutes, then place their journals in a box labeled "Diary" to await Sara's response. Sara imposes no "rules" about length or topic. She responds to the content of each entry and neither edits nor revises the submitted writing.

Sara's children generally present her with entries about one page in length, the predominant topic being accounts of weekend activities. They use a casual and informal writing style. They follow the formal conventions of language and punctuation loosely and do not always observe spelling rules. They ask very few questions, with the exception of inquiries about teacher's weekend. Jane's entry here is typical:

> On the week-end I went Katie's for a sleep-over and her Birthday. I went to a Rebbles hockey game and It was 4,4 in over time and in the 3 min. of over time Rebbles Won. YES!! Rebble fans were very happy. So was i. I helped at the church meal and I was there till 2:00. I slept in till 10:30 and I needed it. I went to Dairy Queen for a treat and then I helped my mom with the garden. I hope you had a good week-end.

Sara and I discussed her impressions of these journal entries, and she told me that

> I use journals for communication purposes and also for children to express their feelings. I think sometimes they express their feelings more honestly in a journal than if you asked them directly. I don't use them for any other great reason. Actually, to be honest with you, I got into journal writing because it was part of that whole language movement.

As she described how she had set up her journal writing program, Sara voiced her concerns about what the children write and the value of that writing:

Most often I get what they did on the weekend, we do it on Monday, or "I went home after school then I went to so and so's house and then we slept over etc. " It sort of goes like this and this is Grade five and they should be writing much better than that. They should be making it exciting and something that someone else would want to read.

I think that journals have their definite drawbacks. [The students] don't pay attention to punctuation, they don't pay attention to spelling, they just write and write and write, and often it is just one great big long sentence. Often it doesn't make any sense, because they know that no one is going to correct it and say this isn't the way you do this.

It is so frustrating because you can't comment on the writing or the spelling or mechanics without making them upset because you are marking their personal work!

Sara dutifully writes her replies each week, but she finds it increasingly difficult to respond:

I know that my messages are rather brief because it takes time. I read them all, they are all definitely read. But what can you say when all they tell you about is their schedule of activities except "It sounds like you were busy." There is not much to reply to.

True, it is difficult to respond to a "grocery list" of events, but can thoughtful comments encourage children to elaborate and provide details and to reflect upon their experiences? Responding to a set of journals can be as time consuming as the act of writing the initial entry. Sara wants her children to write to her, but she does not consider her responses equally important. She questions whether children should receive actual writing lessons on their journal entries and whether that would make the activity more useful. She wants direction, and needs information that suggests alternatives to the current practice. She wants to find a better way to use journals in her classroom and is eager to learn how others use the activity. Sara also expresses a personal vision of what she thinks journal writing should be for her and her students:

Something exciting happens to you on a particular day and you want to express that. Or you have learned something. [A journal can be helpful] even if it is only to tell about that event and why it

is important to you and why it is interesting. It can be about something that you have enjoyed learning about and why you have
enjoyed it. That is what I would really like. That's why they can
write a little bit about the weekend, but I don't need to know all of
that other stuff.

Sara wishes for writing that shows that the students have
taken time to examine and reflect on the issues and events that
shape their lives. But the children in her classroom do not
share their thoughts and feelings in their journal writing. Sara
looks at journals as a place where students might celebrate
their accomplishments and meaning making. She thinks journals should provide evidence of the connections children
make in their learning. She asks how she can encourage
children to write in such away.

I found Sara's questions and concerns valuable to me as I
re-examined the literature on dialogue journal writing. They
forced me to reflect on the ways in which I use journal writing
in my classroom and the reasons for some of my practices.
Sara reminded me of the importance of questioning and continuing the searching for answers. She asked me to explain
what journal writing is about and why teachers find it useful.
She challenged me to defend my use of journals as a way of
learning more about my students. She asked questions for
which I do not yet have all the answers.

Journals and Writing
As Graves (1983) concluded, "Children want to write. They
want to write their first day they attend school" (p. 3). Young
children quickly realize that those "scribbles" are a way to
communicate with others. They want their efforts understood.
They see writing as a way to broadcast the thoughts and ideas
they so readily and capably express in oral conversations. Yet
the writing forms that they are frequently assigned bear little
resemblance to their oral communication patterns.

These writing assignments often focus on the production
of a finished product, a story or essay the teacher wants them
to complete. The topic may be predetermined with the requirements of form and content clearly set out. Emphasis falls on
meeting a mandated standard and the mechanics of writing

play an important role. The teacher forms the audience for the writing and narrative or essays are the most common style. In many cases, students receive responses to their writing only after they have completed the whole product, and this response often takes the form of a grade with brief evaluative comments from the teacher rather than a meaningful dialogue about the piece.

Conforming to expectations like these requires a certain level of knowledge about how written language works and few young children are ready for them. Shuy (1988) observed,

> Writing begins, as far as the schools are concerned, with monologue writing—the formal essay styles (even though this is sometimes referred to as "informal"). One can only wonder why we have been so blind to the fact that this pattern is in direct violation of the developmental sequence of the kind of language used frequently and often successfully by all children—their oral language (p. 77).

Shuy contrasted the ways schools conventionally teach children to acquire writing skills with the way in which they learn to talk. Children learn to talk by dialoguing with another person or by having conversations with several other speakers. Yet in school, the teacher gives an assignment and the child writes it. The topic is teacher generated, not self-generated, as in speech. When we talk, we say what we want or have to say to express our purpose, rather than what someone else has told us to say. We use oral language to pursue our own agendas. School writing assignments almost always ask students to use language to do what someone else wants to get done.

We also treat speaking and writing attempts differently. We expect young children to experiment with sounds, words, and speech patterns, yet we demand a high level of proficiency from beginning writers. What message do we send when children take risks by using different writing styles or by attempting to spell unfamiliar words and our marking schemes focus on their deficiencies instead of applauding their attempts to grow?

How then can we build on the knowledge of language young children have already acquired in their oral interactions? What types of writing would encourage them to rely on this learning? When I look at how children communicate with others, I invariably notice competence. They know how to ask questions and how to build upon the answers to predict, challenge, and applaud. I can see a lot of sense in a format that encourages them to use the knowledge they already possess, one that mirrors in written language the interactive nature of oral language acquisition. In every brief journal entry a child writes, I can infer a literate and interesting invitation from a person wishing to communicate.

Dialogue Journals

Staton (1988a) defines dialogue journals as "written conversations between two persons on a functional continuous basis, about topics of individual (and eventually mutual) interest" (p. 312). These conversations introduce students to an expressive and thoughtful use of writing as they come to know themselves and their world better. Using the term "interactive writing," Hall (1994), defined it as "writing involving the participation of two or more friendly correspondents who exchange meaningful and purposeful texts across an extended period of time" (p. 1).

Dialogue journals are more than just talk written down. A written dialogue may share many relationships with talk, but it goes well beyond simply talk put into writing. Interactive writing links talk with literate language and encourages a gradual move toward mastery of the formalities of literate language. Participation in dialogue writing, while rooted in many of the traditions of oral language, can, as Kreeft Peyton (1988) noted, "provide a natural bridge from interactive communication to the unique demands of essayist writing" (p. 106). By becoming involved with students in communicating on interactive topics, the teacher helps them build on their writing to elaborate and gradually produce extended prose within or separate from the journal. In Braig's (1986) formulation,

> Dialogue journal writing may be an important link between oral language competence and written competence; an oral and written language support where assisted writing occurs before independent formal language writing (p. 111).

Staton (1988b) posited writing in journals as a link between informal conversation and the traditional essay writing so familiar in schools She discussed how at the younger grades journal writing can provide an opportunity for children to develop their abilities as authors as they search for a way to achieve an ongoing relationship with another person, an audience.

The Changes in Sara's Journals

As my study progressed I began to see changes in the entries Sara and her students wrote. The students' entries began to avoid lists of weekend activities and include classroom events and opinions of school activities. Sara's responses lengthened to include references to common activities or previous conversations. When I pointed this out, Sara expressed surprise. She had been unaware of any change in the way she assigned the journal writing. After some consideration, however, she admitted she had encouraged her children to venture beyond weekend activities and had suggested including comments about school events and opinions. The children had begun to address topics that required elaboration and opinions, and these entries demanded a response beyond just "Interesting" or "Nice." Here is a typical pair of entries:

1. I am disappointed in my marks. I guess I need to do more work. But I don't like the assignments we have to do in science.

2. One thing I don't like about school is the way violence is treated. We have zero tolerance for violence policies and yet [they are] not being reinforced. I'm worried for the children who can't self protect themselves. I think children who do violence should be suspended, not given a warning. I was given a warning for going on the ice rink. [But] these kids hurt kids seriously. I think they should be punished severely.

These children are expressing their views, hoping their teacher will honor their opinions and ideas. Sara could hardly avoid asking questions or making comments that show her desire to engage her students on these issues.

The Adult's Role in Responding

Kreeft Peyton's (1988) studies illustrate how students progress developmentally from writing that restates shared knowledge with little new information to explicitly interactive writing that provides information in response to questions the teacher posed. Students then begin to share implicitly interactive writing in which they anticipate the teacher's or an adult reader's questions and provide that information. This progression illustrates the remarkable similarity between the acquisition of oral and written language.

As teachers repeat and rephrase key words and concepts they find in their students' journal entries, they provide what Cazden (1983) called "interactional scaffolding." The adult provides a conversational foothold upon which the learner can step, then a new foothold is provided, and so on. Wells (1986) heightened my understanding of this concept when he commented on how, instead of taking the leadership role, the adult "leads from behind, letting the child take the initiative, while the adult uses a variety of techniques to support and extend the child's topic" (p. 15). These techniques include thoughtful questions and supportive comments.

The importance of interaction in learning was impressed on my mind as I read the work of Vygotsky (1962). He discussed how a child's language development begins in social interaction, and that children begin to direct their own thinking processes only after engaging in social interaction with adults. Children find help in the initial formation of their thoughts and gradually progress to the point where they can express themselves without help. The work of those researchers who have examined the social aspects of writing development confirms the importance of interaction in writing and interaction about writing as children develop written language skills (Graves, 1983; Calkins, 1986; Atwell, 1987).

My Principal Purpose for Journal Writing

I use dialogue journals to keep in touch with my students in a personal way. The classroom time we spend together can be frantic as children move from activity to activity and from place to place with parents and administrators and other adults frequently distracting my attention. I sometimes feel that I never get time to "talk" or "visit" with the children. Our verbal interchanges too often deal with instructions, questions, or exchanges of information necessary to the established routines. We talk about "school things," I ask where their report card or home reading sheet is and where they put their snow pants and toques. At the end of the day, I often feel as though we have only occupied the same space, not sharing it in ways likely to promote my goal of creating a community of learners. We find few opportunities to dialogue on personally important matters. Too often we forgo those conversational opportunities to get down to the "business of teaching." The dialogue journal gives me a way to maintain contact in spite of the demands of the classroom. As Lindfors (1987) wrote, "The classroom is a very special kind of community and requires some special ways of communicating" (p. 372).

Dialogue journals can meet this important need. But to forge that link, both teachers and children must be willing to work together to establish a process that invites them to express their thoughts and ideas freely.

Avi (1987, as cited in Calkins, 1991) insisted that "if you can convince your children that you love them, then there's nothing you can't teach them" (p. 11). In the responses I provide my students I hope to show that I do love them and that their stories matter to me.

References

Atwell, N. (1987). *In the middle*. Portsmouth, NH: Heinemann.

Calkins, L. (1986). *The art of teaching writing*. Portsmouth, NH: Heinemann.

Calkins, L. & Harwayne, S. (1991). *Living between the lines*. Portsmouth, NH: Heinemann, Educational Books, Inc.

Cazden, C.B. (1983). Adult assistance to language development: Scaffolds, models and direct instruction. In R.P. Parker & F. Davis (eds.), *Developing literacy: Young children's use of language*. Newark, DE: International Reading Association.

Eliot, G. (Mary Ann Evans) (1874). *Middlemarch*. London: Backwood and Sons.

Fulwiler, T. (1987). *The journal book*. Portsmouth, NH: Boynton/Cook.

Graves, D. (1983). *Writing: Teachers and children at work*. Portsmouth, NH: Heinemann.

Hall, N. (1994). Interactive writing: Its nature, purpose and scope. In N. Hall & A. Robinson (eds.), *Keeping in touch: Using interactive writing with young children*. Portsmouth, NH: Heinemann Educational Books.

Kreeft Peyton, J. (1988). Why ask? The function of questions in dialogue writing. In J. Staton, R. Shuy, J. Kreeft Peyton, and L. Reed (eds.), *Dialogue communication: Classroom, linguistic, social & cognitive views*. Norwood, NJ: Ablex Publishing Corporation.

Lindfors, J. (1987). *Children's language and learning*. NJ: Prentice- Hall, Inc.

Madden, L. (1988). Do teachers communicate with their children as if they were dogs? *Language Arts, 65*(2), 142-145.

Shuy, R. (1988) The oral language basis for dialogue journals. In J. Staton, R. Shuy, J. Kreeft Peyton, and L. Reed (eds.), *Dialogue communication: Classroom, linguistic, social & cognitive views*. Norwood, NJ: Ablex Publishing Corporation.

Staton, J. (1987). The power of responding in dialogue journals. In T. Fulwiler (ed.), *The journal book*. Upper Montclair, NJ: Boynton Cook Staton.

Staton, J. (1988a). Dialogue writing—Bridge from talk to essay writing. In J. Staton, R. Shuy, J. Kreeft Peyton, and L. Reed (eds.), *Dialogue communication: Classroom, linguistic, social & cognitive views*. Norwood, NJ: Ablex Publishing Corporation.

Staton, J. (1988b). Dialogue journals in the classroom context. In J. Staton, R. Shuy, J. Kreeft Peyton, and L. Reed (eds.), *Dialogue communication: Classroom, linguistic, social & cognitive views*. Norwood, NJ: Ablex Publishing Corporation.

van Manen, M. (1986). *The tone of teaching*. Richmond Hill, ON: Scholastic Books.

Vygotsky, L. (1962). *Thought and language.* Cambridge, MA: MIT Press.

Wells, G. (1986). *The meaning makers: Children learning language and using language to learn.* Portsmouth, NH: Heinemann.

Chapter Eight

Teaching Young Children to Research

Vireo Karvonen-Lee

> To exist humanly is not merely to be in time but to encompass it or "take it in" as our gaze takes in our surroundings (Carr, 1986, p. 95).

> We need curriculum researchers where loyalty to their problems and to the research enterprise is so strong that they would be willing to put their deepest beliefs to test of practice rather than judging practice by the standard of their beliefs (Walker, 1992, p. 115).

I held many unexamined beliefs about children and learning before my advanced studies forced me to examine and reevaluate my assumptions and practices. My research compelled definite adjustments in my thinking and my teaching practices. Carson states that "research should actually improve practice" (p. 2). My teaching practices definitely improved as I researched a genuine concern with my students. The entry question for my interpretive inquiry suggests the nature of this concern: "How can I get my students to conduct research in our new unit on birds without inadvertent plagiarism?"

When I began my inquiry I was prepared to conclude that written paraphrasing (taking notes and doing research without plagiarizing) was too difficult a task for my second grade students, especially in a class of 27. Many futile attempts had almost convinced me. Moreover, I had heard no success stories about such young students developing research skills.

Student Research: Setting the Stage

Schostak (as cited in Ellis, 1994b) suggested that the most important work of teachers is to support students in the formation of life agendas and that "to engage with the life of another we must first listen to the voice of the other" (p. 36). I consider it important to listen both to an individual's voice and to the collective voice. Thus, I began our bird unit by asking my students to brainstorm what they knew and wanted to learn about birds. My approach complied with the general learner expectations from the Program of Studies for kindergarten, first grade and second grade, which expects students to "contribute to the development of group questions that focus the search for new information and ideas" rather than develop questions independently (Alberta Education, G.L.E. 2.2.). To encourage my students to say what they really thought rather than just what they thought would please me, I had them work first in cooperative groups. In addition, to avoid presenting this unit on birds in a self-contained, disconnected way, I asked my students to bring material on birds from home. Like Ellis, (1994b), I wanted my students to feel that their out-of-school lives had relevance in our classroom.

The Research Begins

I began my inquiry by attempting a technique I had discussed with a teacher who, with a full time assistant, taught a learning disabilities class of eleven students. I had more doubts than hope for this technique, but the desire my students expressed to "do research" overcame my skepticism and spurred me onward. The technique involved the following four steps:

1. Read five sentences aloud to the class, in this case about a particular species—the eagle.

2. Ask the students to listen for and write down two or three key words for each phrase, after hearing each phrase only once.*

* A few students were not successful in being able to select any key words.

3. Ask the students to reconstruct their key words into sentences, in their own words.

4. Invite the students to share their sentences individually or collectively.

At first, the individual and collective sharings suggested that the above technique had been successful, but had I stopped there, I would have missed the uncoverings. When I proceeded to ask my students what they meant by certain statements they had created, like "Eagles are birds of prey" or "Eagles are famed," I was surprised to learn they did not understand what they had written. As I engaged some of my students in conversation, I was even more puzzled to find that they had felt successful when they wrote statements they did not understand. This discovery made me realize that some of my students' understandings of reading, as well as writing, remained at a naïve stage. They believed that if they could say or print a word, they were reading or writing (and in a sense they were). From their perception, they were writing key words, reading their sentences, and—behold!—they were successful. At least I understood where my students were developmentally. I had assumed that if they wrote, not just copied something, they would be able to read and understand it. Obviously, I was mistaken. I also realized that many of my students had yet to grasp the importance of understanding in the reading process or the notion of ownership and understanding in writing.

One can already see why I concur with Ellis's (1994a) idea that "through narrative inquiry with a child or youth, one can more clearly and sympathetically understand the young person's motivations, preoccupations, preconceptions, hopes, fears, loves, aspirations, and interpretive frames" (p. 372). By listening to my students, questioning them, and engaging them in conversation, I had already come to a better understanding of their meanings and their frameworks. Had I just focused on a right or wrong answer, or good or bad paraphrasing, I would have missed the opportunity to learn and to deepen my understanding of my students and their individual needs.

Although I had not engaged my students in a pre-planned, formal or lengthy interview process, I came to realize that even short conversations where one or all of the participants are trying to reach a common meaning represent a form of meaningful narrative inquiry. As Weber (1986) stated, "[T]he interview has its best moments when the interviewer and the participant are both caught up in the phenomenon being discussed, when both are trying and wanting to understand" (p. 5).

The children's misunderstandings (from the teacher's judgmental point of view, at any rate) or perceptions caused me to reexamine the texts I had chosen to read to my students. This reexamination led to more uncoverings. I discovered a level of syntax and semantics too advanced for some of my students. For example, for most students, the statement "Eagles are fierce looking birds" became "Eagles are fierce." The students focused on the words they knew and on the task of choosing key words, rather than on the full meaning of the sentence. I understand now that it is also possible the children were constructing their own meanings based on past experiences or myths about eagles. Simpler texts at an easier reading level would make the task of choosing key words easier and more meaningful and would support a better learning experience for my students. This is not to say that I would avoid more difficult and "real" unedited texts once the children had learned the skill of selecting key words in a phrase.

Searching Again, Helped by Two Other Teachers

Conversations with Joyce
When I used simplified teacher-created texts on the whooping crane and penguins, I was bewildered to find that some of my students were still unable to select and record key words during this oral exercise. I was frustrated and unsure where to proceed from there, so I decided to return to Joyce, the teacher who had originally shared the key word technique with me.

My interview with Joyce helped me to appreciate the following statement by Mishler (1986):

> [I]f we allow respondents to continue in their own way until they indicate they have finished their answer, we are likely to find stories; if we cut them off with our next questions, if we do not appear to be listening to their stories, or if we record a check mark or a few words on our schedules after they have talked at length then we are unlikely to find stories (p. 235).

Not only would I have missed the stories if I had not really listened, but I would also have missed deeper meanings, richer connections, and quite possibly the "deeper truths" or the "real answers" to some of my original questions and concerns. Also, Joyce might not have gone so far as to show me samples of student research had I interrupted with too many focus questions. I found being able to *see* what she was talking about in the students' work valuable.

Through our discussions, I came to learn that Joyce engaged her students in a broad range of preparatory listening, reading and writing activities before proceeding with more demanding research tasks. I had been using the key word listening exercises she suggested in a rather limited way. From Joyce's stories about certain of her pupils, I made connections later to some of my own students. For example, one non-reader and non-writer in her class needed someone to scribe for her and then help her reread the scribing. I saw that one of my students would probably require similar assistance. I was surprised when Joyce, an outstanding teacher with 26 years of experience, told me she had one of her students recopy key phrases from the board. A part of me rebelled against this idea. On the other hand, I also realized that with a class of 27, it was unrealistic for me to expect to create individual programs for all of my students. Joyce could not even achieve this with her class of eleven.

Conversations with Frances

To broaden my perspective further, I decided to interview a teacher who currently taught in a fourth grade class but who had previously taught in grades one through five. Frances was gracious enough to share her expertise, a few stories from her own experience, and some promising research techniques.

As Weber (1986) wrote, "In asking someone to participate in an interview, we are thus in a sense extending an invitation to conversation" (p. 1). In order to engage in a productive interview-conversation with Joyce and Frances, I had to set aside my list of questions and agenda, and allow the interview to take on a life of its own and be more like the "invitation to conversation" Weber speaks of. Once I did this, their stories emerged. I agree with Carson's (1986) remark that: "maintain[ing] the openness of the conversation is both an art and a skill" (p. 4). At different times during my conversations with Joyce and then Frances, I found it difficult just to listen and not interrupt with my own ideas.

Both interviews led to uncoverings. I learned that my students needed a lot more than I was giving them, and it became evident that few of them had the skills necessary for the research task I was asking them to complete. From the interviews with Frances and Joyce, I isolated the following three requirements:

1. Some of my students might need more teacher-led modeling on, for example, how to select key words, and how to rewrite key words into a sentence of their own.

2. Some of my students might need examples of other methods of doing research like categorizing, creating headings and color coding according to these categories, note taking and highlighting or underlining key words.

3. Some of my students might need visual examples (on the board or the overhead), hands-on experiences, reader or scriber assistance, more structured or smaller bits of information or a system for organizing gathered information (for example, a labeled page for such categories as appearance, food, habits, babies, and habitat), and more practice.

A New Direction: Examining My Own Teaching

My inquiry seemed to take on a new direction at this point. Rather than focusing on what my students were doing or not doing in their paraphrasing efforts, I had to reconsider and expand some of my own teaching methods. Until that moment, I had assumed that if my students could choose key words from an oral or written text they could also independently use these skills to conduct their own written research project. I am amazed to realize only now as I write this chapter, that prior to interviewing Joyce and Frances, I had assumed that my students would just be able to "do research." I had failed to recognize the complexity of such a task and was surprised that I had not previously thought of some of the common sense ideas in the previous list on my own. I had to view the task from the students' perspective and look at how they might approach it or might need to have it broken down and simplified for them. Accordingly, my students and I approached the research work again.

I returned to the original idea of having the students select key words, but this time I gave each student a copy of a teacher-created text on penguins. As I modeled the procedure and followed the step-by-step diagram I had drawn on the board, the students discussed and explained why certain words would be good choices for key words and why others would not be.

5 key phrases ——

  1. ——underline key words——

   2. ——write key words on separate paper——

    3. ——write 5 new sentences with key words——

Before we could proceed further, I knew I also had to go back to the beginning and build a framework for the students to work with—a context for learning and new meanings. It seemed as though many of them needed a step-by-step recipe of instructions to follow since they had never done research before, just like someone who has never before baked a cake. As a class, we went back to our brainstormed questions about what we wanted to learn about birds. With my help, the students created categories and sorted the questions into these categories. I was surprised at how easy this task became for

them once we came up with a system for organizing the questions. The system had meaning because they had personally
helped create it. I displayed our questions on large strips on
the bulletin board. They identified similar questions and
proceeded to create headings for groups of questions. Once
they had agreed on the headings, they gave each heading a
code letter and color: A for appearance, B for babies, F for
food, H for habits, E for environment (or habitat), and II for
interesting facts or information. The students were then able
cooperatively to color and letter code the strips of questions.

The New Researchers Emerge
With this scaffolding to build on, my students and I worked
with a selection of texts in a teacher-created photocopied book-
let on different species of birds. First, we focused on a text
about the robin. I displayed information on the overhead
while the students used their individual booklets to underline
our agreed-upon key words with the appropriate color code. I
was pleased to discover that many of them could rewrite these
key words independently into expressive and informative
texts. Since I was teaching a very specific skill, I had not
expected such individuality and open-endedness in the re-
writing task that followed the group work. All of their paraphrasing and rewritten paragraphs about the robin were so
unique and different, both from one another's and from the
original text—all this even though we had all selected the same
key words. The following unedited pieces of writing about the
robin illustrate how diverse and original the children could be
in their common writing about the robin, even when they
worked in the same group.

The Robin by Carlyn (gr 2)

robin's have red brest's and
they are beautiful too. They can jump
over the ground looking for earthworms
in the spring. His nest is made of
grass, rootlests and mud, the robin sits
in the nest and terns rond and
rond, and makes a beautifully cup-

shape with his brest, and it lases
three to five bluish eggs in a season.

The Robin by Clayton (gr 2)

1. A Robin has a redbrest.
2. Today I saw a robin.
3. A Robin is beautiful.
4. The Robin gos south when
   winter comes.
5. a Robin is very fast.
   I know becaues I trid to cach one.

Following the activity with the robin text, the students
worked in groups with texts about the flicker and the red-
winged blackbird. Taking turns, they read the texts aloud, para-
phrased each paragraph orally, then identified and underlined
key words in each paragraph. Once they agreed upon key
words, each student used them independently to write his or
her own paragraph about the flicker and the red-winged
blackbird. Since they still sat with their groups, they could
help each other in their individual tasks. Once again, I had not
expected to see such personal styles and individuality emerging in this type of paraphrasing, especially since each group
used the same key words. For example, Ryan used phrases
such as "I'll tell you about . . ." and his own words like
"sweet" to describe the robin's song. Heather began her
paragraph about the robin with "our friend robin Redbrest."
The play with style is obvious in Kelsey's example.

The Flicker by Kelsey (gr 2)

We know the bird
that stars with a "f."
It's a flicker! The flicker
is big and strow. He has
a resob belty of getting food.
He is in the Woodpecker
flimy. He's grate! I
love the flicker!

Most of the words from Kelsey's sample, even "responsibility" (resob blety), come from outside the original text about the flicker. To my surprise, the writing task was open-ended enough for Kelsey to express and compose her own piece about the flicker, freely incorporating her prior knowledge, at her own higher level of ability. Kelsey's writing about the flicker, as well as the work of the other students, brought me to agree with Kerby's (1991) view that "language plays an integral, even constitutive, part in almost all of our dealings, with the world [and that] language is viewed not simply as a tool for communicating or mirroring back what we otherwise discover in our reality but is itself an important formative part of that reality, part of its very texture" (p. 2). I realize that my students' oral and written language is a big part of their reality and helps define who they are as individuals.

Although I believe in cooperative learning, I hardly expected the learning that took place in the cooperative groups to be so heightened and rich. Vygotsky's familiar idea that "What we can do today with help, we can do alone tomorrow" definitely received reinforcement. Students working cooperatively to read and discuss paragraphs with their peers almost eliminated direct copying and greatly increased the level of comprehension and success.

During my inquiry I also noticed with Ellis (1994b) that "the children's related values, beliefs, preconceptions, and preoccupations" emerged more readily in the small group, cooperative learning setting (p. 35). The students had more and better opportunities to share stories, make connections, and negotiate and construct their own meanings. In this way, the learning that took place exceeded my expectations. This success and pleasure supported my role as a guide helping students discover, rather than a bestower of knowledge. After much modeling and practicing, most of the students could pursue their own research projects either independently or with a partner. They were less dependent on me; they felt free to interact with their groups.

Some students still experienced difficulty, however. Danielle's paragraph about the robin indicated that the unusual wording and phrasing of some of the texts still posed difficulties for students who struggled in reading and other areas of language arts. In her writing sample about the robin, Danielle interprets "The Robin is never more beautiful than in the spring" as the opposite of what it means. In this situation, the focus on selecting key words may have detracted from the importance of understanding and preserving the meaning of the original text. Unfortunately, I had no time to dialogue with Danielle. Doing so would have helped me see from her perspective. It would have also allowed me to determine whether or not she was alert to the meaning of her words. But Danielle taught me an excellent lesson in the importance of keeping my students from getting lost in a specific task and of helping them to look at their own and each other's writing more globally in order to check for sense making.

Danielle (gr 2)

> The Robin has a redbreast.
> The Robin is not that
> beautiful in the spring
> time. The Robins like
> earthworm very mach.
> The Robin is more
> numerous than over birds.

I surprised myself at how involved I could become in the correctness and coherence of a piece of writing rather than focusing more on the process of the individual student, in this case Danielle. Danielle's and other students' writing samples reminded me of the truth in Garbarino's (1992) observation that "a critical problem for all interviewers of children is understanding the meaning of children's statements" (p. 198). I would add that understanding the child's intended meaning in written statements is probably as difficult, if not more difficult, than in oral statements.

The Story Continues: New Research Directions
In the course of my study I made many discoveries and came to better appreciate the learning taking place in my classroom. I am grateful for the chance to make connections, to make

sense of certain aspects of my teaching, to construct my own understandings and reality, to bring new and deeper meaning to my experiences, to deepen my understanding of myself as teacher and learner, to deepen my understanding of my students, and to perceive my students and their learning from a new viewpoint. In six weeks of research, I saw what Peshkin (1993) called "the feast of possibilities that may result from qualitative research" (p. 23). I would also agree with Peshkin that as researchers we should search for understanding, rather than for absolute "truth." As Kerby (1991) noted, "[T]he value of an event is dependent upon how we narrate that event" (p. 12) and the form of research I describe here allowed me to narrate my own "event" or journey. In the same way, if we keep students from articulating their own stories, making connections between what they already know and what they are learning, or narrating their events "and bringing meaning to these events" there may be little value in what we teach or they study. As Sarbin (1986) made clear, "[M]eanings are constructed only when the context is taken into account" (p. xv). As teachers, we must help students create contexts for their learning or allow them to create their own contexts. Without meaning, learning is lost.

To conclude, I can affirm that second grade students can, indeed, conduct research. But that simple affirmation understates what I learned from my interpretive inquiry. At the same time, I have barely touched the surface, even though I shed some light at different angles and in different areas on some complex issues related to children's learning. To quote Peshkin again, "Clarifying and understanding complexity. . . is important because most of what we study is truly complex, relating to people, events and situations characterized by more variables than anyone can manage to identify, see in relationship, or operationalize" (p. 27). I consider my qualitative research "good" because it widened my perspective and sent me searching further. As Barton and Lazarsfeld wrote, "[R]esearch outcomes that lead usefully to subsequent research are invaluable" (as quoted by Peshkin, p. 26).

This work has inspired me to examine narrative inquiry. When I reflected on the research processes underway in my classroom, I was disappointed to see that too many opportunities for storying were lost. I know stories were being shared during class discussions, during cooperative learning, and as the students consulted each other during their research, but it disturbs me to know that I put so little emphasis on them. Robinson and Hawpe (1986) both enlightened and frightened me with these observations: "Narrative thinking—storying—is a successful method of organizing perception, thought, memory, and action . . . it is *more effective than any other* [emphasis added]. [Yet] personal anecdotes offered by students during discussion or questioning [are] rejected by teachers as inappropriate" (p. 123). This disturbs me because I have occasionally rejected students' stories or cut them short when interrupted by more immediate demands.

In a system where teachers already feel overwhelmed by testing and curriculum expectations and where class sizes increase rather than decrease, how can I continually engage in productive narrative inquiry with my students and take time to listen to their stories? Sarbin (1986) defined loneliness "as the inability or refusal to share stories with others" (p. xv). As disturbing as it is, I agree with him. I would add only that in today's classrooms, loneliness stems from a system that silences students' stories, rather than a refusal on the part of the students to share their lives. I have yet to meet a student who has no story to tell.

References

Carr, D. (1986). *Time, Narrative and History*. Bloomington, IN: Indiana University Press.

Carson, T. (1986). Closing the gap between research and practice: Conversation as a mode of doing research. *Phenomenology and Pedagogy, 4*(2), 73-85.

Ellis, J. (1994a). Narrative inquiry with children: a generative form of preservice teacher research. *International Journal for Qualitative Studies in Education, 7*(4), 367-380.

Ellis, J. (1994b). Student teachers researching students in social studies. *Canadian Social Studies, 29*(1), 34-37.

Garbarino, J., Stott, F., and Faculty of The Erikson Institute. (1992). *What children can tell us: Eliciting, interpreting and evaluating critical information from children*. San Francisco: Jossey-Bass Publishers.

Government of Alberta, Alberta Education. (1991). *Elementary Language Learning Program of Studies*.

Kerby, A. (1991). *Narrative and the self*. Bloomington, IN: Indiana University Press.

Mishler, E. (1986). The analysis of interview-narratives. In T. Sarbin (ed.), *Narrative psychology: The storied nature of human conduct* (pp.233-255). New York: Praeger.

Peshkin, A. (1993). The goodness of qualitative research. *Educational Researcher, 22*(2), 23-29.

Robinson, A. & Hawpe, L. (1986). Narrative thinking as a heuristic process. In T.R. Sarbin (ed.), *Narrative Psychology: The storied nature of human conduct* (pp. 111-125). New York: Praeger.

Sarbin, T. (1986). *Narrative psychology: The storied nature of human conduct*. New York: Praeger.

Walker, D. (1992). Methodological issues in curriculum research. In P. Jackson (ed.), *Handbook of research in curriculum* (pp. 98-118). New York: Macmillan Publishing Co.

Weber, S. (1986). The nature of interviewing. *Phenomenology and Pedagogy, 45*(2), 65-72.

Chapter Nine

Double Vision: Negotiating the Roles of Teacher and Researcher

Susan Hart

> Poems can give you
>
> Poems can give you
> double vision.
> They make you see
> the colours you feel
> when you're sad,
> the sound of a red,
> red sunset,
> the smells of happiness,
> the flavours of the seasons,
> Double vision
> not blurred
> but crisp as last night's snow.
>
> —Sandra Bogart

Introduction

For three years, I taught in an elementary school close to the inner city. The local neighborhood was made up of older homes, apartment buildings and low-rent townhouse complexes. Businesses around the school included a liquor store, a gas station and an adult video store.

Most of the students lived in the immediate neighborhood. Many lived in low-rent apartment or townhouse complexes and came from single parent families on welfare. Some had been Child Welfare or other Social Service clients. On several occasions police had entered the school to question children where abuse had been suspected, and on at least one occasion, took a child out of school and placed him in foster care.

The students in the school came from varied racial and cultural backgrounds. Many were Native Indian, or had recently come from countries where English was not spoken. Some came to us from refugee camps in war-torn countries. Many could tell horror stories of their homeland.

School suspensions were abundant and children from grades one through six had been suspended for up to a week (some repeatedly) for willful disobedience, for carrying knives, for setting fires in the bathroom garbage cans, and for preying upon other students after school. Many of the children accepted and even preferred violence for dealing with problems on the playground and elsewhere.

I spent the 1994-95 academic year as a teacher-researcher in this school. My part-time teaching assignment included music, health and physical education for grades one through six. My research required me to spend several mornings or afternoons per week in the sixth grade classroom observing and talking with students. My goal was to document the children's perspectives of schooling in the hope of improving my understanding of their lives both within and beyond the classroom. I wanted to find ways to help them achieve personal growth and gain learning. I hoped as well that their knowledge and perspectives would inform and guide my own teaching practice.

When I think about the year I spent researching, I have mixed feelings. Perhaps inevitably, I found no magical way to learn the "children's perspectives." It certainly isn't as easy as simply asking them, "So, how do you feel about school anyway? What experiences have been the most remarkable for you?" But I do think their perspectives depend on how they view the situation, who is asking the questions, and why they are being asked. They have a kind of double vision: Who is this woman who teaches us music on Friday afternoons, who disciplines us and humors us and bribes us with parties and then shows up in our classroom Monday morning and sits and watches and talks to us with her tape recorder on and then ignores our bad behavior?

Teacher and Researcher as Oppositional Roles

Who was I, teacher or researcher? The academics rarely treat this duality as problematic. "Teacher-research," they call it, as if you could somehow bring these two very different classroom stances into a comfortable union. Cochran-Smith and Lytle (1990) defined "teacher-research" as "systematic, intentional inquiry by teachers about their own school and classroom work" (p. 84). I found being a teacher and being a researcher quite different. Teaching was well defined and understandable, something that had been amply modeled for me throughout my school career. Research was none of these things. And the only models I had to guide me came from the pages of research journals or books. As this journal entry shows, I found it difficult to marry these two ways of being:

September 29, 1994

> *I am finally finished my proposal and once I get it presented, I will be able to "officially" begin my research. I have been visiting the grade six classroom on an occasional basis. The students have begun to show their "true colors." I am disturbed by my reaction to them. When I am teaching, I have little patience. I am trying to develop a more patient approach, but I have such a hard time reconciling my "job": that is, trying to TEACH something with the attitudes and behaviors the kids bring to the classroom. When I am spending time in the classroom as a researcher, I am much more laid back, I don't feel stressed about the students' behavior, I am just enjoying being in the classroom and interacting with them. Why is there a difference? Is it because when I am the TEACHER I feel more accountable than when I am the "researcher"? Could be.*

My role constantly shifted from teacher to researcher and then back again. I wondered what I was doing, who I was supposed to be and how the students might be making sense of my chameleon act. I began to question my teaching. What did it mean to be a teacher and why did it feel so different from being a researcher?

Throughout the course of the year, I continued to question. My research changed from trying to make sense of the children's perspectives to trying to make sense of my own:

January 29. 1995

My research is changing, so it seems. I am preoccupied with who I am as a teacher, and I have somehow realized that the students don't provide the answers I seek. I suppose that they provide a lens that I can look through—or perhaps it is just that their behavior makes me want to reach them, I don't know. I am afraid of this shift—is it "academic" enough, does it contribute to the conversation that is already within the educational community, can it help others to learn about my struggle with who I am as a teacher? I don't want to focus only on myself in my research. I suppose though, that the time when we looked for answers outside of ourselves is over, and now is the time to look inward. Not that we should become preoccupied with our own experiences, but we need to begin in who we are and what we believe before we can look outside ourselves to find new ways of understanding what we see and do. Perhaps my work is to find out how my own experiences resonate with the experiences of others, with the research that has been already done in education, to RE - search: search again.

The next three stories offer a window into my experiences as a teacher-researcher and illustrate the double vision that occurred in my teaching as a result of looking carefully and seeing in a different way.

The Music Specialist

I was the "music specialist" at the school the year of my research project. That meant I taught music to the classes whose teachers either had no musical training or declined to teach music. Grade six was always a challenge. How do you motivate students with musical activities of at least some sophistication when they have little or no musical experience? I tried all kinds of activities and used every behavior modification technique I could think of. Yet some students remained perpetually challenging, regularly disrupted my lessons, and introduced chaos into the music room at every available opportunity. What to do? More often than not, I simply asked the disruptive students to leave.

As my frustration mounted, I worked up the courage to call the music consultant from the school board. I was afraid she would ask to observe my teaching and then critique it. But she offered instead to teach the class while I observed, and I readily agreed. Watching her teach, I saw responses from the students I had never seen before. Her teaching techniques resembled mine, and the curriculum she followed was the one I had been using. The difference was in her attitude and behavior toward the students. I was amazed at the transformation that began to take place:

January 29, 1995

> *I have been thinking about what my current preoccupations are. My first idea was my music teaching. I am excited about the possibilities, I look forward to teaching those children who I previously had problems with and I have begun to see the potential for learning in these kids. They are musical! They can create music! When the consultant came in, I saw a class of grade sixes I had never seen before. They were enthusiastic, they participated, they did things I never would have dared try. I wonder. . . why were they behaving differently? I suppose that a large part of the reason is that the consultant expected them to be excited and participate. I, on the other hand, often enter the classroom expecting the worst: Will I get through this lesson without a major power struggle? Will Jason and Kevin decide to act up? Will the students be bored? I am coming to understand in a very real way just how large an impact my enthusiasm, my attitude and my expectations have on the way the students react to a particular situation or lesson. This should be nothing new; after all, I learned it in introductory educational psychology—only then it was in a text book and it was theory—now it is in my classroom and it is real.*

With double vision, I began seeing myself through the eyes of the students. I examined what I was doing, how I was teaching, and seeing in a different way, I changed my approach and attitude towards the class:

February 1, 1995

> *Music with the sixes. It was a good day. They are very musical. I am somewhat concerned about evaluation, because I don't do any formal evaluation but I will try to be patient with myself. This too will come—with some time, effort and energy. The real successes are the students. They are excited and motivated—and so am I!*

Together we are accomplishing so much. And without all of the
CONTROL I thought was so vital. Thinking back, I think my idea
of control was that everything had to be in a set, certain way, and
if only there were consequences for everything, they'd learn. I felt
that if I let go even a little, chaos would result. I've discovered this
isn't true. While there are still routines and guidelines, the con-
sequences are small and non-alienating—the children do not get
angry and hostile, and they know that the choice is theirs to make.
Once they are invited back into the group, they know it's a clean
start. This works so well with them. There simply is no anger
anymore. I think after Spring Break I will do away with the
behavior book and the marble jar. It will be interesting to see what
happens.

I had learned an important lesson about how to share classroom space with students and how strongly my behavior and
attitude could influence theirs. But it was one thing to know
this and quite another to carry it through to the end of the
year. I often lacked the energy to sustain a positive, energetic
classroom environment. The students I was trying to reach out
to continued to push me away. I felt like I was caught fighting
against a current that ran far beyond the music room.

The questions continued, and eventually I learned to
accept that this too was part of that process called teacher-
research, that I was bound to find more questions than
answers.

The Friday Morning Writing Class

Part way through the first term I was asked to teach a Friday
morning adaptation class, a few fifth and sixth grade students
who spent half of every day in a small group in order to get
remedial help in math and language arts. The class already
had a teacher, but she was available only Monday through
Thursday. To give the students a full program, the administra-
tion added Friday morning to their adaptation schedule.
During our Fridays together, we focused on writing.

When I began teaching the Friday morning class, I had no
preconceived agenda or method for teaching writing. I intended simply to excite them about writing and engage them
in enjoyable writing activities rather than dry and routinized
assignments. At times it was difficult to ignore what I would

have previously considered "off task" behavior and let the students write in their own way and in their own time. I had no behavior expectations, other than that it be reasonable and not disturb the work of others. There were no consequences for not writing on any particular day except that unfinished writing would not appear in our class book. Nevertheless, with time and patience, I began to see the students as emerging writers: they were beginning to write for themselves, and they were beginning to enjoy it.

My approach to this class was unlike any other approach I used in my previous four years of teaching. Because I had been considering and questioning my role as a teacher and the impact my behavior and attitude had on my students, I wanted to make the classroom "child-centered." For me, this meant letting go of my own expectations and letting the students find their own way in their own time. Since many of the students also had behavior problems, I considered it important to adopt a broader definition of "acceptable behavior" than the structure I usually imposed. It was a difficult and sometimes uncomfortable adjustment. My beliefs, attitudes and philosophy about teaching and children continually changed as I struggled to preserve my goals. I found the pressure strong to lapse into my traditional ways of teaching. Ironically, rather than coming from outside, this pressure came from within as I questioned what it was I was doing and whether or not it was benefiting the children in any way. My doubts appear in this long journal entry:

February 27, 1995

Last Friday morning, things were uneasy. I am thinking that perhaps I have lost my focus, or that I am changing the way I want things to be in there. Perhaps the children sense it and they are rebelling against it. I don't know. I gave them a writing "assignment." I wonder now if that was a mistake. It was supposed to be used for me to look at and compare to their other writing this year in order to come up with some kind of evaluation for their report cards, but I didn't rely on the samples very heavily. In fact, Rita didn't even hand one in, although she promised to by this Tuesday. I'll be surprised if she remembers. Despite not having her assignment, I completed her report card comments anyway. I feel

like such a hypocrite, and I wonder how much damage I've done by re-introducing this "traditional classroom" junk into the sanctity of the Friday morning environment.

I am worried about that room, and I feel as though the kids aren't "progressing" because I'm not doing any structured work with them. I haven't been having individual conferences with them, and I don't write in red all over their work. What is it that I have been doing? It feels like nothing much, it doesn't take the energy of a traditional classroom approach (maybe because I'm not always fighting with them to sit down and get to work??!!). I think that what I've been doing is introducing activities at the beginning of every class that I'm hoping they will transfer to their writing. Talking about character, setting, description, sequence, problems in stories, point of view, "real life" stories— is this enough? I am back to the curse of "the teacher"—shouldn't I be giving written tests, with percentages? Shouldn't I be showing these kids how to improve their work in a more direct way? Ahhhhhhh!!!!! I think about their other teacher and her "first year teacher" perceptions. I feel guilty that I don't "enforce discipline" in that classroom, because it makes it more difficult for her to get CONTROL of the students and make sure they are ON TASK and DOING THEIR WORK. I have explained my perspective to her and she seems okay with it, but I often have these visions of her going home to her boyfriend and complaining that the only time these kids have structure and control and expectations is when she's in there. And it makes me feel GUILTY that someone may be judging me like that, guilty enough to make me think of changing what I do in that classroom. Are they progressing? Are they learning? If so, what? And is it learning I can see? If not, is that okay? There are no easy answers here, just more and more questions.

Next time I am with the students, I will stop pressuring them. Writing is fun, it is enjoyable to express yourself and to share that expression. Every student in that class has written something *and I must trust that what I am doing is the right thing. It certainly feels right, even if it doesn't look right or even sound right. Some of the students do respond to the idea that I may be EVALUATING a particular piece of writing, and those students do their best. But it is not the students who are turned off, and these are the students I want to try and reach. Every so often, I see a glimpse of a miracle, and those days are wonderful. I wonder if I am expecting too much too soon.*

Another thought has just come to me: Is it unfair of me to teach these students in such an open environment, one devoid of the pressures of marking and evaluation and traditional classroom management and traditional definitions of work? This may be the only time they are allowed any sort of freedom in the classroom from here on in. When John and Rita and Amber get to Junior High and (hopefully) high school, what will become of them? How will they have found the strength to believe in themselves, in what they can do? It certainly isn't being fostered in their present environment. And, they have turned off, and are either openly defiant, like Rita and Amber, or passive and resigned, like John. I am afraid for these kids. I don't want to let them down. I don't care about giving them skills or coping strategies or phonics or formal sentence structure; I just want to give them the will to succeed, the will to keep on trying, the belief in themselves. Some kids already have that, but there are so many here who don't.

I am proud of what we accomplished in our Friday morning class. We published two class anthologies and wrote and performed puppet plays for the first grade students. Although their writing did not noticeably improve in form or mechanics, nearly all of my students became more confident, fluent writers. A few exceeded my expectations and made me wonder how they had reached the adaptation class in the first place.

When I think about my experiences with the Friday morning class, the writing seems almost incidental. The learning that occurred in there had more to do with developing a sense of community and finding a safe place to learn in than with anything else. If I am really honest with myself, I can admit that I did not really care about the writing all that much; I found it far more important to give the students a sense of belonging and a belief in themselves. Writing made less of a difference than the time we spent baking cookies, playing in the gym and talking about ourselves. They all had the comfort of knowing that when they had bad days they could sit and be alone and no one would mind; they had the comfort of knowing that I expected them only to be themselves and no matter what they accomplished, I would accept and like them.

With my double vision, I often pushed aside my impulse to release the reins of control and just let the students find their own way. I often felt constrained by the mandated curriculum, the standardized testing, and the "discipline policy." I often felt like a failure because "good teachers know how to make the curriculum relevant and interesting to students." It is hardly enough to be a "good teacher" when the students in your classroom have not had their basic needs met, when they feel alienated, and when they define themselves as failures.

The Friday morning class provided an opportunity that simply does not exist in a regular classroom situation. Because the students were in an adaptation program, no formal marking occurred; the report card was anecdotal and without letter grades. Each student followed an individualized plan with learning goals, specified at the beginning of the year, based on past accomplishments. Of course, these individualized plans were just academic window dressing and failed to address the social or emotional needs of the students in any meaningful way. With double vision I found myself working within a system that does little or nothing to help students like these, while for one morning each week, I actually could do something to help them.

The Math Centers

As I began to examine the role I played in the Friday morning adaptation class, I began to think about ways I could incorporate some of my approaches there into the regular grade six classroom. I recorded some of these ideas into my journal:

February 20, 1995

I need to write about the things I have been thinking about and the direction my research is now going in. I thought about why the Friday morning class seems so much more productive and fruitful than the regular classroom and I came up with the idea that one major difference is that there is no such thing as failure. Further to that, I am now in the process of creating some math centers for the sixth grade room where I will try to incorporate this idea. The centers won't be marked and there won't be any competitive edge to them, no pressure to complete a certain amount by a certain time, etc. The students will be allowed to help one another, although they will all be responsible in some way for their own work. The only rule is that they may not interfere with the work of others, either directly or indirectly. This may mean that some students don't do anything at all in the centers, but I think that most of them at least will attempt something or other. I have tried to make them interesting enough that the students will want to try out the activities. I believe that the very same students who don't participate in traditional classroom instruction may also opt out of the centers. It just may be more obvious here, and take a slightly higher tolerance level to accept that some students are choosing not to work. I believe that good things will come of this.

The idea of using centers to teach sixth grade math was exciting and daunting at the same time. What content would I cover? How would I ensure enough centers to engage all 28 students at one time? What would the regular classroom teacher think of my plan?

The classroom teacher agreed to participate and I decided to focus on problem solving, an area that the students needed to work on. This problem solving focus also allowed me to create a wide variety of centers. Because of space restrictions, I created centers that were mobile—that is, even when the students had to work with manipulatives, they were portable and moved easily from one part of the room to another. Each center was housed in a box labeled to provide easy access and efficient clean up. Each student had a sheet to chart his or her progress through the centers. When a student completed a centre, he or she received a stamp. If corrections were required and completed, the student received a second stamp. No grades were awarded for work done at the centers; they simply used the stamping procedure.

Before we began working, I explained to the students that I had designed the centers to help them improve their problem-solving skills: I would dispense with marks; they could help one another; and no pressure existed for them to complete all of the centers. The only rule was that no student could interfere with another student's learning. We began working at the centers and wonderful things happened:

February 27, 1995

I introduced the math centers to the grade sixes. I was pleasantly surprised at the amount of work some students completed. More than that, I was surprised that they followed my lead and actually tried to figure things out on their own. I only saw one student put something down and say it was too hard. Even Kevin and Jason were giving some honest effort.

> *Some of the students had gone to our school's annual garage*
> *sale (never to return) and so the class was significantly smaller*
> *than usual. I am curious to see how it all falls together (or apart)*
> *when everyone is there. Rita said to me, "I have to do MATH*
> *here?" I matter of factly said, "YES" and she accepted it. She did*
> *one center during the time and was successful at it. I wonder what*
> *kind of impact this could have on her self esteem?! I suspect it*
> *must feel awfully nice to be able to succeed at math in the "regular"*
> *classroom when you are taken out of that setting every day for half*
> *of the day.*
> *It was okay. I was okay. The classroom teacher was okay. The*
> *kids were moving around, they were talking and chaos did not*
> *reign supreme. We all survived and the students actually learned*
> *something (I think)—or at the very least, they were thinking and*
> *sharing and getting along. School was fun for awhile, I think??*
> *Imagine, learning that doesn't feel like learning. It makes me*
> *wonder how we've been defining things.*

The math centers engaged the students, encouraged them
to help each other, got them talking about math, and helped
them learn. Even the students who normally studied math in
the adaptation class successfully completed some of the centers. For me, the math centers provided a vision of what a classroom could look like when students were free to move and
talk and work at their own pace, and when the focus was on
learning rather than evaluation.

More double vision: authentic, genuine learning versus
straight rows and dry textbooks. Yet the tension remains: What
about the test? Have I covered the mandated curriculum? What
about discipline? What about control?

Looking Forward, Looking Back
When I began my research, I thought I knew where I was
headed. I thought I had drawn an accurate map and that even
if I got lost, I would still be able to find my way. I thought that
research would fit fairly neatly into my life without a lot of
adjustment. I thought a "right" way to "do research" existed
and that if only I had more experience, I would discover what
that was. I wanted to be a researcher, I wanted to feel like a
researcher, but I had yet to occupy the position:

March 7, 1995

I have not yet defined myself as a researcher, I do not yet have a vision of what it looks like or feels like to be a researcher, I have not carved out a space for this research, or rather, it has not carved its way into my life. I hear the words echoing, "Maybe it's not your time." It must be my time, I ache for it to be my time, I want to think and learn and write. Why then, have I not been able to see myself as a researcher? To have a vision of what it is to be a researcher? To feel like a researcher? Is it that I have not given myself permission? Must I be selfish to do this thing called research? I know it is an uncomfortable, ambiguous process—I think I have accepted that—but what of being a researcher? I am asking the same questions over and over. When I am reading, many thoughts go through my mind, not just thoughts related to my teaching or my research, but creative thoughts. I have strong urges to write stories, to paint, to create somehow on a page. How does this relate to my research or to who I am as a researcher? I push these thoughts aside or else I cannot read any longer. I want to run upstairs to my computer and write a story or a poem. I want to draw large pictures with charcoal or paint, I want to create, I want to express. I don't know if research is for me. Can I create? Meaning, certainly, but is it the same? I ache to create, yet when I sit down to do it, I am often disappointed. I think this may be because it hasn't yet carved itself into my life. I want to give myself over to these things, yet I cannot. Real life gets in the way. What has this to do with my research?

Over the course of my research year, I often experienced frustration with how my project was proceeding. I thought that if only I could schedule research into my life, it would go relatively smoothly. I was wrong. I had failed to anticipate, for example, that I would lose all of December because of the immense amounts of time and energy required to put on the school Christmas concert. I failed to anticipate buying a house and moving during the months of April and May. Most of all, I had failed to anticipated that my style of working and thinking and writing simply did not fit into tidy blocks of time. Moreover, instead of accepting and embracing this reality, I fought it. I despaired that I was being insufficiently "productive." I felt alone and disoriented:

March 9, 1995

*I have set aside this time to write. Now what to write? I often feel
as though the only time I can write is when I am inspired to do so.
If I wait to be "inspired" all of the time, this research will take an
awfully long time. That's okay, too. I have accepted that I may not
be done when I wanted to be done—as long as I am still moving
forward (and backward, Gadamer might remind me) I can feel at
peace (sort of) with what I am doing. I suppose it was foolish of
me ever to think that I could "fit" research into some concrete
block of time in my life, not if my work is to have the kind of
meaning I want it to have. This idea of blocks of time is becoming
a recurrent theme in my life and in my thoughts. It is a difficult
thing to let go of, not only in my teaching, but in the rest of my
life as well. I have always felt that I could plan things, and for the
most part, my plans have worked out fairly well. I suppose
though, that research cannot be planned in the same way. And not
just the research itself, but the entire "life-space" that the research
and the researching and I as a researcher entails. I'm not sure if that
makes any sense, but at least it approaches explaining what I feel
about this process.*

In the years since I wrote those journal entries, I continue
to wonder what it really feels like to be a researcher. I am
learning that being a researcher simply is not as concrete a
position as I first imagined; rather, it becomes part of who you
are. It is not some kind of label you assume in the
"academy," it is a way of being in the world. I suspect that
teaching should be this way too, although it never was for me.
Or maybe it is impossible given the constraints of our current
educational system.

I spent a year away from the classroom, studying full time
at the University. When I left teaching to become a full-time
student, my vision seemed to clear. I saw less ambiguity and
confusion. My role was more clearly defined. My memories
of the classroom seemed to fit more neatly with all I was
reading and thinking about.

I know now that this clear vision itself is just an illusion: a
product of not having to negotiate between the two worlds of
the researcher and the teacher. It is a result of not having to
accommodate the contradictions that invariably enter classrooms and schools. It is a result of not having to deal with the

limitations of educational discourse within government policy, a discourse that pays lip service to educating the "whole child" but focuses squarely on learning objectives, evaluation and outcomes.

I still find more questions than answers. But I have learned that research is not about putting things into neat compartments or recommending procedures for complex tasks like teaching. It is not about explaining how or why strategies work, although the positivist language of teaching and research often make it sound as though this were the case. It is about merging perspectives and finding new ways to understand what transpires in classrooms and schools. It is about paying attention to the sensory and the emotional, not just the intellectual. It is about seeing the "colours you feel when you're sad," hearing a "red, red sunset," smelling happiness, and tasting the "flavours of the seasons." It is about cultivating double vision and accepting that the world will occasionally go out of focus.

References

Bogart, S. (1989). Poems can give you. In D. Booth (ed.), *Til all the stars have fallen: Canadian poems for children.* Toronto, ON: Kids Can Press Ltd.

Cochran-Smith, M., & Lytle, S. L. (1990). Learning from teacher research: A working typology. *Teachers College Record*, 92 (1), 83-103.

Gadamer, H-G. (1976). *Philosophical hermeneutics.* Los Angeles, CA: University of California Press Ltd.

Index

narrative portrait, 36, 42, 53;
   writing of, 41
Native Indian, 148
natural sciences paradigm, 29
needs, 67
Noddings, N., 90
notes, 100
nurses, 24
nutrition, 60, 63

objecitivity, 30
objective reality, 8
optimism, 87
Ottawa, 31
outcomes, 161

Packer, M., 15, 22, 26, 28
Paley, V., 81, 87
paradox, 92
paraphrasing, 133, 141
parents, interviewing, 43, 44;
   interview schedule, 54
participant-observer, 100
patterns, 41, 65, 74
pedagogy, 76
perspectives, 161
Peshkin, A., 144
Peyton, J., 126, 128
plagiarizing, 133
play, 58, 65, 66, 75
poems, 147
political views, 42
Polkinghorne, D., 44
positivist: languages, 161;
   research paradigm, 7
possibilities, 29
post-positivist tradition, 7
postmodernism, 8, 9, 81, 92,
   94
Potter, J., 44, 45

practicum, 70
praxis, 57
prejudices, 8, 26
problem solving, 157; skills,
   157
procedures, 75
program goals, 85
psychiatry, 35
psychology, 34, 35
punctuation, 122
punishments, 88
purposes, 26

qualitative research, 100, 144
quantifiable data, 7
questions, 29; entry, 18, 19,
   21, 133; focus, 137;
   probing, 52

reading, 103; difficulties, 97,
   98; remediation lessons,
   98; strategies, 105, 107
reflection, 6, 32, 36, 42, 53,
   88
reflective practice, 81
relationships, 41, 45, 114
relativism, 8
report cards, 84
research, 7, 29, 57, 58, 84, 85,
   98, 99, 108, 149, 158,
   161; methods of, 138;
   participant, 29; procedure, 99; process, 9, 159;
   reports, 12; student, 134,
   139; teachers', 6, 152;
   work site, 7
researcher, 101
resources, 93
responsibility, 9
risk, 91